BILLY WILLIAMS

My Sweet-Swinging Lifetime with the Cubs

Billy Williams and Fred Mitchell

TRIUMPH
BOOKS

Triumph Books and colophon are registered trademarks of Random House, Inc.

Library of Congress Cataloging-in-Publication Data

Williams, Billy, 1959-
  Billy Williams : my sweet-swinging lifetime with the Cubs / Billy Williams with Fred Mitchell.
    p. cm.
  ISBN-13: 978-1-60078-050-9
  ISBN-10: 1-60078-050-4
  1. Williams, Billy, 1959- 2. Baseball players--United States—Biography. 3. African American baseball players—Biography. 4. Chicago Cubs (Baseball team) I. Mitchell, Fred. II. Title.
  GV865.W49A293 2007
  796.35709--dc22
  [B]
                                        2008001908

This book is available in quantity at special discounts for your group or organization. For further information, contact:

Triumph Books
542 South Dearborn Street
Suite 750
Chicago, Illinois 60605
(312) 939-3330
Fax (312) 663-3557

Printed in U.S.A.
ISBN: 978-1-60078-050-9
Design by Chris Mulligan
All photos courtesy of Billy Williams unless indicated otherwise.

CONTENTS

FOREWORD

Billy Williams and I hold the record for the most games played together as major league teammates. So I believe it is only fitting that I continue to stand by the side of my lifelong friend and teammate by writing the foreword to this autobiography.

I first met Billy during a three-week Cubs rookie camp in Mesa, Arizona, in 1958. I was 18 years old and it was the first time I had been away from my hometown of Seattle. The players in this special camp were considered to be the top 30 rookie prospects in the organization.

The moment I met Billy, I just felt as if I had known him forever. We felt very comfortable around each other; Billy and I just hit it off. The two of us spent a lot of time together those three weeks. We always hit in the same batting group, and we hung out together after practice.

Billy had been in the minor leagues already for a couple of years, and Rogers Hornsby was our batting instructor in the camp. I was in awe of Hornsby because I knew he was a Hall of Fame player, a terrific hitter.

At the end of the three-week camp, Hornsby had us all sit in a small bleacher area. Billy and I were sitting next to each other as Hornsby went down the first line of players and told each one of those guys that they wouldn't get past Class AA ball. As he is telling them that discouraging news, Billy and I are looking at each other, worrying and wondering what he is going to say to us next.

Hornsby turned to Billy and said, "You can hit in the big leagues right now!"

As I am sitting next to Billy, I am thinking, "Oh, please, don't tell me to go home."

Hornsby turned to Billy and said, "You can hit in the big leagues right now!"

But then Hornsby said to me, "And you can hit in the big leagues."

Billy and I were the only two position players who made the big leagues out of that group. I came up to the big leagues in 1960, and Billy came up in 1961 and was the National League Rookie of the Year.

In 1959, Billy and I were teammates with the Class AA San Antonio Missions. One day in the middle of the season, our teammate J.C. Hartman came over to me and said, "Ron...Billy went home!"

I said, "What?"

Billy was having a great year at San Antonio. I was hitting behind Billy in the batting order, and we were both having good years.

It wasn't until later that I realized just how much discrimination Billy and the other black ballplayers on our team were facing.

When we played in Texas and traveled to different small towns in that state, our bus would stop before we got to the team hotel and let Billy off. I couldn't understand it, being from Seattle, Washington. I asked Billy, "Why are they dropping you off?"

Billy said, "They won't let me stay in a white hotel."

I felt so bad. It really made me sick to my stomach.

That's when the Cubs called Buck O'Neil to track down Billy in Whistler, Alabama. He was back with our ballclub in about a week.

Whenever Billy or I found ourselves in a little bit of a hitting slump, the team called in Hornsby. He would look at us and always say, "Remember what I told you. Stay back in the batter's box and take a short stride." That's all he said. He never messed with our mechanics.

It wasn't until later that I realized just how much discrimination Billy and the other black ballplayers on our team were facing.

Throughout our careers in the big leagues, Billy and I used to watch each other at the plate. We used to be our own hitting instructors.

I hit behind Billy in the lineup. And whenever he would walk up to the plate, before he stepped in the batter's box, he would spit out his gum and hit it with his bat in midair. Or sometimes he would spit and hit it with his bat. He would never miss! I would try it and couldn't do it.

Everybody in the media thought that Billy was extremely shy when he was a young man. But in the clubhouse with his teammates, he was a leader. Billy spoke his mind, and I loved that about him. On the field, he very seldom would argue with anybody. He would just keep hitting line drives. I have never seen a left-handed hitter in my life as good as Billy Williams. I really mean that. He could hit a pitch at the last second and take it out of the ballpark. Sweet Swingin' Billy had a gift that allowed him to wait on the ball like no other hitter I have ever seen.

I was named captain of the Cubs at the age of 23. And I thought that to be an honor. But I always thought a captain was one who did the job with the bat and the glove when it came to setting the example. In that sense, Billy Williams was a leader on our ballclub. Kenny Holtzman also was a leader. Fergie Jenkins was a leader. Glenn Beckert, Randy Hundley...you could just go down the line.

Billy spoke his mind, and I loved that about him.

But what I loved about Billy is that if he had something to say to somebody, he would go right up to that ballplayer and have a one-on-one with him. Billy was beautiful about that. I think that is why all of us on that 1969 Cubs team remain so close, even though we did not make it to the World Series that year. All of us care about one another. Billy will be always special to me. He is a very lovable guy—a caring guy.

We were a very entertaining ballclub in '69. We had three Hall of Famers, and we related well to the fans. We posed for pictures, and we knew that when we walked down by the left-field line at Wrigley Field, we would all sign autographs. We said "hi" to everybody. It was a wonderful love affair.

Back in those days, the players' families were close and not that many guys from the nucleus of our team got traded. When we did get traded, it was at the end of our careers.

The Cubs Fantasy Baseball Camps that Randy Hundley has been conducting for more than 25 years in Arizona have been a great way for all of us to keep tabs on one another. The great thing about those reunions is that we can all embellish a lot of our stories. And believe me, there are some really strange stories that come up.

But this book is filled with remarkable, true stories. I know because I was right there, kneeling down in the on-deck circle, watching the life of Sweet Swingin' Billy Williams unfold.

—Ron Santo

CHAPTER 1

I Quit!

I am taking the first train out of here. Heading back home to Alabama. Baseball just isn't any fun for me anymore.

That was my mindset in 1959 when social conditions and racial tension at Class AA San Antonio, Texas, left me weary, angry, and frustrated. Sad thing was, I was tearing the cover off the baseball then, hitting around .320, and playing well, challenging Carl Yastrzemski for the Class AA minor league batting title. That's where I first got the nickname "Sweet Swinging Billy Williams."

But I was not accustomed to being treated like an animal away from the baseball diamond. I couldn't take the bigotry, discrimination, and overt racism.

Back in my hometown of Whistler, Alabama—just outside of Mobile—black people and white people lived in the same neighborhoods, frequented the same stores and restaurants. Sure, there was a level of discrimination, but much more subtle. My mother worked for white folks as a domestic and had no problems. I tried to understand the rules of segregation in San Antonio, but I certainly didn't like them.

I would help entertain fans at the ballpark by playing baseball to the best of my ability, but then I was not allowed to eat in their restaurants or stay in their hotels. My black teammates and I had to rely on our white teammates to bring us a sandwich in the back of the bus after they were done enjoying their casual meal in a segregated restaurant. Jim Brewer, a white pitcher who befriended me in the minors, often made sure I got some food delivered to me. He later pitched in the big leagues and enjoyed some success, playing 17 years with the Cubs, Dodgers, and Angels. He died tragically in a car accident in 1987 at the age of 50.

The South Atlantic League, the Carolina League, and the Texas League were among the several minor league systems that were not fully integrated until 1964. It took several demonstrations and boycotts by black fans in the South before players of color were more widely accepted and treated with more respect. And, of course, it took the enforcement of civil rights legislation by the federal government in the 1960s to really force the action.

The Carolina League was first integrated in 1951 by a ballplayer named Percy Miller Jr. who played for the Danville (Virginia) Leafs. I helped integrate the Texas League after future big leaguers Manny Mota, Felipe Alou, and Hank Aaron had spent time there in the early- and mid-'50s.

Ed Charles, who was a member of the 1969 World Series champion Mets, played nine years in the southern minor leagues and withstood incredible discrimination and the sanctions of Jim Crow in the South.

Our minor league team was called the San Antonio Missions, which had previously served as the Class AA affiliate of the Baltimore Orioles. The Missions became associated with the Cubs in 1959, but only for a four-year period of time. Unfortunately, I was a member of the Missions at the start of that time frame when race relations had not yet evolved. Nowadays, San Antonio is the largest metropolitan area without baseball at the major league or Triple A level. The Missions are now the Class AA affiliate of the San Diego Padres.

The despicable and inhumane treatment got to the point where I couldn't take it anymore. I shared my frustration with my roommate and teammate, J.C. Hartman, who had gone through the same type of treatment as I had.

I said, "J.C., take me to the train station. I don't want to stay here anymore."

That comment hit J.C. like a ton of bricks. He knew how much the game of baseball meant to me and to all of us on the team.

Finally, he confided, "Billy's gone home and he's not coming back. Billy said he can't take the abuse anymore."

J.C., who was born in another small town in Alabama named Cottonton, said, "Why? Are you going home? I'm not doing that. I'm not taking you to the train station."

We argued back and forth until I finally convinced him that I was leaving, whether he took me to the station or not. So J.C. drove me there and I said, "I'll see you later," when he dropped me off, even though I had no plans at the time of ever returning.

Grady Hatton, a former big league infielder who played for 12 seasons, was our manager in San Antonio in 1959. After I left the ballclub, he asked J.C., "Where's Billy?"

J.C. found it very difficult to tell Hatton where I was.

Finally, he confided, "Billy's gone home and he's not coming back. Billy said he can't take the abuse anymore."

Hatton then immediately called Cubs general manager John Holland back in Chicago.

Meanwhile, I sat back in my seat on the train headed to Mobile on that blistering hot summer day, sweat dripping from my forehead and my shirt drenched with perspiration. There was no air conditioning on that train, yet I thought to myself, "Damn, I feel good."

I told my dad I would rather get a job back home doing pretty much anything else than to go through the humiliation I was going through in San Antonio.

When I finally arrived in Whistler, I stood in front of our house, which had 75 to 80 steps leading up to the front door. We lived in an area of our close-knit community known as "Baptist Town."

The only other person I had told about coming home was my older brother, Franklin. I am one of five children, and some people considered Franklin to be the best athlete of the family. When I had talked to him on the phone from San Antonio, he kept saying to me, "The fish are biting and the weather is great." Those inviting comments made me want to come home even more.

But I kept wondering what I was going to say to my father. After all, he and I used to sit glued to the television, watching Major League Baseball games and always talking about my dream of one day becoming a big-league ballplayer.

We had a screened-in porch in front of the house and my father was sitting there, just rocking. He looked up and was surprised to see me at home, of course, with my suitcase in hand. I immediately told him that I couldn't stand it in San

Antonio anymore. I told him about the discrimination, about how the black ballplayers were the first ones picked up in the wee hours of the morning and the last ones to be dropped off at our separate hotel after the games.

I told my dad about the incident in Corpus Christi, Texas, when J.C. Hartman and I tried to eat in a restaurant. The guy behind the counter said: "We will feed you boys, but you have to go back in the kitchen to eat."

At first, my father got on me a little bit about quitting baseball. He said, "You've got an opportunity to do something with your life."

I told my dad that all the black ballplayers were driven across the tracks to a beat-up building called the Manhattan Hotel, while the white players were allowed to live in a much nicer facility.

It was his dream to see me one day make it as a big-league ballplayer to escape the cycle of unfulfilled promise.

I told my dad I would rather get a job back home doing pretty much anything else than to go through the humiliation I was going through in San Antonio. He said he understood, but I could tell he was hurt and disappointed that I was giving up on a dream. Our dream.

It certainly was not as if Whistler, Alabama, was any great majestic mecca. But it was home to me. It was my comfort zone. My hometown, by most objective accounts, was an impoverished southern outpost near the dock of the bay, not too far from Mobile. But it was rich in terms of beautiful people, beautiful trees, and beautiful memories.

There were shabby boarded-up shanties, desolate dirt roads, and abandoned shelters converted into churches, where the inner strength, faith, and purposefulness of the humble congregations belie the frailty of the makeshift structures.

Elder residents in my hometown still know me as "Jessie May's Boy," and I return periodically to pay my respects. My mother, the former Jessie May Moseley, passed away in 1977 and my father, a former sandlot ballplayer of some local renown, called our old Williams residence at 2939 Pyton St. his home until the day he passed away.

Black ballplayers of the past had already made huge sacrifices so that players like me could even have a chance to play Major League Baseball, including the legendary Jackie Robinson.

In 1987 my grade school principal, Mrs. Lilly A. Dixon, passed away. I mentioned her in my Hall of Fame acceptance speech. She always talked about the "good, better, best" idea. My high school football coach, Virgil Rhodes, passed away. And the lady who delivered me passed away. She was 93 years old. My father passed away when he was 92 years old. He lived a good, long life, and he got to see me perform in the major leagues. He enjoyed what I enjoyed.

I suppose, looking back now, that my father had suffered and endured a great deal more discrimination and humiliation than I had when he was a young black man growing up in the South. It had not occurred to me at the time that he must have had so many dreams deferred because of racism and segregation. It was his dream to see me one day make it as a big-league ballplayer to escape the cycle of unfulfilled promise. No doubt he lived somewhat vicariously through me and my brothers during an era of enhanced opportunities, even though they presented themselves in relatively modest terms in the late 1950s in America.

John Holland had been pretty close to my family. I had been to spring training with the Cubs the previous year, so he knew who I was.

Holland previously had been involved with the minor league Oklahoma City Indians of the Texas League when he inherited them from his father in 1936. In 1942 he sold that club and went into the Army. After his discharge, Holland became general manager of the Los Angeles Angels of the Pacific Coast League. Then he came over as the Cubs' GM in 1956, taking the place of Wid Matthews. Holland served as the Cubs' general manager from 1957–74 before serving in other management positions in the organization.

So you can see, Holland was quite familiar with the way things were done in the minor leagues in the South during those days.

Right away, Holland knew to call Buck O'Neil, the legendary scout who had touted and signed many black ballplayers, and said, "Hey, we've got a good player in the organization by the name of Billy Williams."

Buck said to Holland, "I know who he is. I have been to his parents' house and I have sat around with them. And I have even eaten at their house."

I was spotted originally by O'Neil, the same eagle-eyed talent seeker who discovered my friend and former Cubs teammate Ernie Banks, also a Hall of Famer. Ivy Griffin later signed me to a contract when I was just 17, just two days after I finished high school in 1956. I turned 18 a couple of weeks later. I got $1,500 to sign. That's when I reported to Ponca City, Oklahoma, and stayed at a family's home. I also befriended Bobby Walton in Ponca City. There were four of us black ballplayers who stayed at this family's home. I got a big room in the front of the house. Future Cub players Lou Johnson and Sammy Drake also stayed in that house. When the rest of the older players went on the road to play games, they left me at home. We played home games at Conoco Park and I got five or six pinch-hits. I remember that they gave us $2.40 a day for meal money.

Being away from home for the first time, I saw a lot in Oklahoma. I went to rodeos and met a lot of new and fascinating people.

I advanced to Double A San Antonio in 1959 and that is where the discrimination really started to unnerve me. I remember I was on a bus coming from Albuquerque, New Mexico, thinking about my life and what I was going to do. I remember saying to myself, "Is this what life is like outside of Whistler, Alabama? Will I be subject to this kind of treatment wherever I go? Life seems so much simpler back home."

Holland told Buck to drop everything he was doing right then and go down to Whistler and find out what was wrong with me.

My wife, Shirley, and I were going together at that time and Shirley was mad at me because I didn't call her to tell her I was quitting baseball to come back home. Shirley grew up in nearby Plateau, Alabama. Buck arrived in Alabama about two days later. I was sitting on the steps of the porch, and I looked up and saw this car coming. Buck always drove a Plymouth Fury. I noticed it wasn't an Alabama license plate; it was a Missouri license plate. So I am thinking that I am really in trouble now.

But I was trying not to give it a second thought. In my mind, at that moment, I wasn't going back to San Antonio. No way.

At first, Buck didn't say much. He simply said, "How do you feel, boy?"

I said, "I'm doing pretty good, Buck."

Buck said, "Got a call yesterday from John Holland. The Cubs think a lot of you. You're playing good; you're hitting the ball good. They think that one day you might be in the major leagues because your scouting reports are good. What do you think?"

I said, "Buck, I have had enough. I don't want to go back there anymore to play any baseball. I have enjoyed the time that I played. But I just don't want to go through the stuff that I have been going through off the field. You know, waiting for the white guys to bring me sandwiches, staying in separate run-down hotels, and things like that."

In fact, I credit Robinson as a baseball pioneer who opened the doors for all players of color—not just African Americans—to play in the major leagues.

Buck knew all about the discrimination in those days. I wasn't telling him anything he didn't know himself firsthand. He had experienced it himself throughout his entire life. Buck also had managed the Kansas City Monarchs of the old Negro Leagues, and he had a lot of players who had been homesick and wanted to go home. But I repeated, "No, I am not going to go back to San Antonio."

At that point, Buck said, "Okay," and then he talked to my dad before he went back to his hotel. The next day, Buck came back over to our house and we talked again. It must have been around 3 or 4 o'clock in the afternoon.

There was a place down there in Alabama called Prichard Park. That's where all of my colleagues and guys who were in my class went to play. And that is where I spent many hours playing ball myself over the years. They happened to have a game going on that night. That afternoon, at my house, Buck said to me, "Come on, boy. Let's take a ride."

I am proud to say that I followed Jackie's path by being named NL Rookie of the Year in 1961 and eventually also joined him in the Hall of Fame.

I had always played sandlot baseball in neighborhood clearings such as Prichard Park and Mitchell Field. I remember local legends around there such as Ed Tucker, the owner of an area semi-pro team; Edward Scott, who later scouted for the Boston Red Sox; and Jessie Thomas, who scouted and signed Hall of Fame slugger Willie McCovey for the San Francisco Giants.

By about 6:00 or 7:00 we made it down to Prichard Park, where the guys naturally were playing baseball. Buck hadn't said much to me in the car about me wanting to quit professional baseball. We were just riding and talking baseball in general. Once we rolled up into the park, everybody there recognized Buck as a big-league scout. Then people noticed I was with him and they started pointing and saying, "There's Billy! Hey, how are you doing? You've been off to play ball, right?"

I said to them, "Yeah, but I'm home now."

Then the fellas said, "Wow! How did you get a chance to play pro ball? How did you get an opportunity to sign and play professional baseball? I bet it's great. Man, I bet you are having a good time playing baseball, doing something you always wanted to do."

One of the guys reminded me of the times we would hit home-run balls that would break the windows in the house of Simon Brown, who lived just beyond the right-field fence at the ballpark. Instead of getting mad at us for breaking his windows, Simon Brown would always say, "I predict one of you guys will play in the big leagues."

Buck just shook his head up and down at everything those guys were saying to me at Prichard Park. You could tell he was loving that influential kind of talk from my friends. He could not have scripted their comments any better. There must have been 10 or 12 guys saying things like that to me, making a big deal about me playing professional baseball. At that point, I started looking around at the guys from my hometown. Most of them were scuffling, trying to make ends meet, trying to make it with scarce job opportunities around town.

At that point, I said to myself, "Well, you know, baseball ain't that bad. And waiting to get a sandwich at the back of a bus from a teammate isn't that bad."

Still, I knew that becoming a big hit outside of Whistler was going to be no minor feat. Black ballplayers of the past had already made huge sacrifices so that players like me could even have a chance to play Major League Baseball, including the legendary Jackie Robinson.

When I was a kid growing up in Mobile, the Brooklyn Dodgers and Cleveland Indians used to come down there to play exhibition games. I got a chance to see Jackie Robinson. I didn't meet him at the time. Then when I came up with the Cubs on August 6, 1959, Jackie was working for NBC and we used to talk about baseball around the batting cage. But I guess the most significant time that I saw Jackie was when the Operation PUSH organization had a day for him at their headquarters in Chicago.

Afterward, a Chicago doctor had a big party for Jackie and his family and I was there. I can remember looking at Jackie and his hair was as white as snow. He was in a wheelchair and I guess he was about at the end of his time. When I looked at that individual and I knew the history of what he went through after playing the game of baseball and coming up in the minor leagues...you begin to see the scars and the stuff he had to endure.

> The older players took care of me, taught me the right way to play baseball. It made me a better ballplayer, going up against men who were five or 10 years older than me.

I signed a contract nine years after Jackie became a Major League Baseball player. With all of the stuff I had to endure, I knew he had to be a strong individual to go through the stuff he did. He had a strong mind and a strong will because he knew that everything was on his shoulders. Jackie believed it was a great opportunity for him.

Pioneering black ballplayers such as Larry Doby, Monte Irvin, and Jackie made it possible for minorities to play in the big leagues. Black players back then had to be good enough to be stars. There were no black players on the bench in those days.

Many people have been made aware of what Jackie had to endure in the big leagues when he broke the color barrier in 1947 with the Brooklyn Dodgers. But I have come to know the many problems he suffered as a minor league ballplayer as well. At UCLA, he became the first athlete to win varsity letters in four sports: baseball, basketball, football, and track. He was named to the All-America football team in 1941. He was forced to leave college because of financial reasons. Eventually he decided to enlist in the U.S. Army. He was court-martialed because of his objections to incidents of racial discrimination, but in the end he left the Army with an honorable discharge.

In 1945 Jackie played one season in the Negro Leagues with the Kansas City Monarchs.

On April 18, 1946, in Jersey City, New Jersey, Jackie's Montreal Royals played the Jersey City Little Giants. Jackie made his minor league debut and became the first black man to play integrated professional baseball in the modern era.

He had just come from spring training in Florida, where he had received some horrendous racial attacks and even death threats.

Jackie and his teammates had been locked out of a game in Jacksonville, Florida, and he had been taken off the field by authorities in Sanford, Florida, because local ordinances prohibited mixed-race games. Jackie also had to endure the rides in the backs of buses, separate lodgings, and the racial slurs.

According to reports of the Jersey City game, Robinson got four hits in his first minor league game, including a three-run homer. He also stole two bases. Robinson had just gotten married on February 10, 1946, and he and his wife, Rachel, desperately needed the money to survive. So they put up with a lot of abuse.

Jackie Robinson won the International League batting title with a .349 average in 1946. In 1947, with the Dodgers, Robinson was Rookie of the Year in the National League. He was NL MVP in 1949, when he led the league with a .342 average.

I am proud to say that I followed Jackie's path by being named NL Rookie of the Year in 1961 and eventually also joined him in the Hall of Fame. In 1961, I hit 25 homers and drove in 86 runs in only 146 games, while batting .278. I wonder what kind of money that would have earned me in today's baseball market!

Jackie retired from baseball after the 1956 season. A severe diabetic, he died of a heart attack in 1972, a year after his son died in an automobile accident.

I think the gesture of having a Jackie Robinson celebration on April 15, 2007, with a lot of the players wearing the No. 42 was important. It gave a parent an opportunity to let more individuals know about Jackie and what he meant to baseball and what he meant to the American people—to let them know that there were no blacks in baseball before 1947.

In fact, I credit Robinson as a baseball pioneer who opened the doors for all players of color—not just African Americans—to play in the major leagues. Robinson was born in Cairo, Georgia, to a family of sharecroppers. His mother, Mallie Robinson, raised Jackie and her four other children as a single parent.

Minnie Minoso was one of the first black Latin players to come over in 1949. Then Vic Power in 1954, Roberto Clemente in 1955, and others.

Minoso was known as "The Cuban Comet" and he was the first White Sox player to break the color barrier in 1951.

Minoso hit a home run in his White Sox debut in 1951 against the New York Yankees. He finished his rookie year as the American League leader in stolen bases and triples.

But Jackie broke the barrier for all people of color; a Latin kid or a kid from Korea or Japan. It would be great if we all recognized what he did. This should be a thing that everybody celebrates because everybody in baseball highly respects what he did.

When I came through the base-ball system in the late 1950s, the odds of me and my contemporaries making it seemed at first to be just about insurmountable. We had no baseball team when I was in high school in Whistler and the facilities **If it weren't for Buck O'Neil, my entire life likely would have turned out differently.** at the school were not good at all. All the black kids had to go to Mobile County Training School and if you wanted to go to college and play ball, there were few opportunities at that time.

Like the rest of the Mobile County Training School students, I was required to wear a white or blue shirt and a black tie every day, even though our parents could barely afford to dress us. Seniors wore red ties to distinguish themselves from the underclassmen. In-school discipline and respect for the teachers were understood.

I played football in high school. I was a skinny 150-pound offensive end and defensive back. Coach Rhodes would always tell us to do the most we could and try to reach our optimum level. If that's not good enough, tough.

But when it came to baseball, I had to play with and against older young men in amateur leagues throughout the area. That is how I learned the fundamentals of baseball. I was only 15 or 16 years old, unable to drive. So men would drive by my house to pick me up and take me to ballparks to play amateur games. They would swing by and honk their horns. My mother would make them come into the house and talk to them first. She would look them dead in the eye.

"Remember," she would say, "you are responsible for Billy. You make sure he is safe and that he doesn't get into any trouble. And you are responsible for bringing him back home safely after the game."

I show that scouting report to some of the black ballplayers today, just to let them know how far we have come and what kind of stereotypes we had to endure.

Only then would she let me go play baseball. The older players took care of me, taught me the right way to play baseball. It made me a better ballplayer, going up against men who were five or 10 years older than me. That's how you learn and get better.

After that memorable session down at Prichard Park with my friends from the neighborhood, reminiscing about our early years of playing baseball, I think Buck was satisfied. Buck brought me back home and we got to talking again. He convinced me that I should go back to San Antonio. I realized this game of baseball was my profession and I was making good progress. And I should stick it out. Buck told me that I might not be in Double A for long the way I was playing, and pretty soon I could be in the big leagues. At that point he had convinced me to go back.

Several other guys from our area received big-league contracts, but they didn't want to leave home. My brother,

Franklin, signed a professional contract in 1955, and I guess he inspired me to play baseball. We used to have many conversations about how nice it was playing ball for money. I said, "That's what I want to do."

Meanwhile, sportswriters from San Antonio had been calling me, wondering if I was coming back. Marvin Milkes was the general manager at San Antonio then. I remember having to go into his office to talk to him after I decided to return on a flight from Mobile. He said, "Well, you're back with the ballclub now. We are glad to have you back. But we have got to fine you some money."

At that time, I told him that if he fined me, I would catch that same plane back that I came up here on. He said, "Well, we've got to do it. I will tell you what, we will tell the press that we are going to fine you, but we won't do it."

He knew that I would jump on that plane and go back home otherwise.

As it turned out, I played in San Antonio another two or three weeks, and then I was called up to Triple A, where I caught up with the team in Denver. I stayed at Triple A for five days and I hit .476. Then in about a week I was on the big-league roster. I only got five hits in 33 at-bats in 18 games with the Cubs in 1959. But it was great to finally make it to the big leagues and I really felt at home there.

I don't know if they moved me through the system so quickly to make me feel good, or because I was swinging the bat so well. But you normally don't get a reward like that.

I know one thing for certain, and that is that the shortage of black major league scouts today is a significant factor in the dearth of black players in the league today. John Jordan "Buck" O'Neil was one of a kind—a terrific baseball man, a teacher, a coach, a mentor, a father figure, and a friend. If it weren't for Buck O'Neil, my entire life likely would have turned out differently.

Someone gave me a copy of a scouting report from Ivy Griffin, who was a white scout for the Cubs in the 1950s. I still have it at home. It reads, "Good-looking colored boy from a good home."

As recently as 1961, when I was a rookie, there were still places black people could not eat in the Phoenix area.

I show that scouting report to some of the black ballplayers today, just to let them know how far we have come and what kind of stereotypes we had to endure.

There was another scout who wrote, "He may not make it out of 'A' ball." That was because I had trouble catching a fly ball early in my career. Obviously, I polished my defensive skills by the time I reached the big leagues.

Yet another scouting report read, "He has a hitch in his swing, but he is making good progress."

Griffin, who lived in Mobile, died in a car accident in Gainesville, Florida, in 1961, my rookie year with the Cubs. His relatives said Griffin was on a scouting mission when he apparently fell asleep at the wheel before crashing. He had been a player and manager as well as a scout. In the early 1950s he scouted for the Cleveland Indians. He was a true baseball man who loved his many jobs in the sport.

In addition to Banks, O'Neil signed George Altman, Gene Baker, Francisco Herrera, Elston Howard, J.C. Hartman, Connie Johnson, "Sweet Lou" Johnson, Satchel Paige, Hank Thompson, and Bob Thurman.

O'Neil, who died October 6, 2006, at the age of 94, became manager of the Kansas City Monarchs in 1948, guiding them to league titles in 1948, 1950, 1951, and 1953. In 1956 he was hired by the Cubs as a scout. As a scout, he discovered Lou Brock and Joe Carter. In 1962, while still with the Cubs, he became the first African American coach in the major leagues.

O'Neil won batting titles in 1940 and 1946 with the Monarchs with averages of .345 and .350, respectively. That he is not in the National Baseball Hall of Fame is simply astonishing to me. His contributions as a pioneering player, manager, scout, and friend of baseball go beyond compare. It truly saddens me to know that he will never know just how much he was appreciated by those whose lives he affected, including mine.

I just hope that what I had to endure has made it easier for those minority ballplayers who have followed me into the big leagues.

A 12-person committee was commissioned in February 2006 to render final judgments on Negro Leagues and pre-Negro Leagues figures for the Hall of Fame. Everyone thought he was a lock to make it with his credentials.

But O'Neil was left out as 16 other men and one woman were voted in. O'Neil was one vote short of the required three-fourths.

In anticipation of O'Neil being selected, several hundred of his friends and well-wishers had gathered at the Negro Leagues Baseball Museum in Kansas City, Missouri, for what they thought would be a celebration. Instead, they stood in awkward silence.

But good old Buck tried to lighten the mood.

"Shed no tears for Buck," he said to the crowd. "I couldn't attend Sarasota High School. That hurt. I couldn't attend the University of Florida. That hurt.

"But not going into the Hall of Fame, that ain't going to hurt me that much, no. Before, I wouldn't even have a chance. But this time I had that chance.

"Just keep loving old Buck."

I was outraged, as were most of his friends and associates.

"It is clear the Baseball Hall of Fame has made a terrible error in not inducting Buck on this ballot," Missouri Congressman Emanuel Cleaver said. "It is rare that an entire community rallies around a single person, but our city loves Buck, what he stands for, and his indomitable spirit. Buck O'Neil is a man who has done more than anyone to popularize and keep alive the history of the Negro Leagues."

I second that emotion.

Shirley and I got married in 1960 while I played for the Triple A Houston Buffaloes. Life was getting better off the field, but there were still too many instances of discrimination. During spring training in Mesa, Arizona, for example, Shirley and I had to stay in Tempe, a suburb of Phoenix, in a beat-up hotel that we referred to as a hut. Meanwhile, my white teammates lived more conveniently in Mesa. There was a little refrigerator and a bed where we were housed, and that was about it.

As recently as 1961, when I was a rookie, there were still places black people could not eat in the Phoenix area. The places we tried to rent would tell us, "We don't mind, but our clients mind."

It was tough. I remember former Cubs player Andre Rodgers and his wife would cook for us quite a bit in 1961.

We all tried to make the best of the situation. The black ballplayers would play pool at the local Elks' Lodge. During spring training, the San Francisco Giants also trained in the Phoenix area, so Willie Mays would often join us to shoot pool. And he was pretty good. Then, sometimes, we would all go together to the dog tracks in Phoenix. We had a midnight curfew during spring training, so we had to make sure we didn't break that.

Even in 1962, when the Cubs played in Houston, we faced discrimination. Houston's team was known as the Colt .45s back then. Our Cubs team stayed in a hotel right near the ballpark. The Cubs' traveling secretary, Don Biebel, told me and the other black players—George Altman, Lou Brock, Rodgers, Banks—on the team that we could not go down to the hotel restaurant and eat. Unbelievable! But that's what we had to endure in those days.

When we played our home games in Chicago, I was able to connect with a black man named Bill Robinson, who played in the Negro Leagues and grew up with my father in Whistler, Alabama. He and his wife would make us feel right at home. After the games at Wrigley Field, Bill and his wife often would invite Shirley and me over to their house on the South Side and fix us a good down-home dinner. I made only $6,500 that first year in the big leagues, so a free meal every once in a while was greatly appreciated.

My first year with the Cubs, I was living in a small apartment right near the "L" train tracks at 69th Street and Stony Island Avenue, on Blackstone Avenue. I had no air conditioning in the unit—couldn't afford it. Then I moved over to the Mansfield Hotel, off Stony Island. I remember always grabbing a bite to eat at a popular place called Ted's

Diner. Our group usually would include Tony Taylor, who played second base for the Cubs, and Banks.

Taylor was a terrific big-league second baseman whose 19-year major league career began with the Cubs. As a native of Cuba, he was forced to endure a lot of the same indignities that African Americans suffered because of the color of his skin. Taylor played with the Cubs in 1958 and '59 before being traded to the Phillies midway through the 1960 season.

Unlike many of the outspoken black athletes today in all professional sports, we had to bite our tongues back in the 1950s and '60s for fear of reprisal from the powers that be. Even though black Cubs players such as Banks, Fergie Jenkins, and I were future Hall of Famers, we knew that somehow our livelihoods were at stake if we made a big public commotion in that era.

Jackie Robinson encountered discrimination and was angered and frustrated by it. He never spoke out early in his career because of an agreement he had with Dodgers executive Branch Rickey. But he did at the end of his life.

Jackie had talked about getting more black coaches on the field in the major leagues after O'Neil broke that barrier in 1962. And Jackie also wanted to see the first black manager. Three years after Jackie died, Frank Robinson became a pioneer as the first black manager (of the Cleveland Indians) in 1975. Robinson also wanted to see blacks become part of management. The late Bill Lucas became a general manager of the Atlanta Braves in 1976. Then Bob Watson took that same position with the Houston Astros in 1993. Today, Ken Williams is the general manager of the Chicago White Sox, who won the World Series in 2005.

I will never forget an important statement Jackie Robinson once made that really applies to what I went through early in my professional baseball career, and what I have tried to accomplish since then. He said, "Life is not important except in its impact on the lives of others. The feeling that an individual who is committed and will persevere can make a difference is part of his legacy."

I just hope that what I had to endure has made it easier for those minority ballplayers who have followed me into the big leagues.

CHAPTER 2

1969 Collapse

Every Cubs fan, especially those who followed the team in the '60s, is familiar with the ill-fated 1969 season. We had a big lead in the National League East as we headed into August. But then our once-comfortable division lead started slipping away—slowly but steadily—like money from the hands of an overzealous Las Vegas gambler.

By late August of 1969, the media covering the Chicago Cubs began questioning the tactics of our obstinate manager, Leo "The Lip" Durocher.

"All of your home games are in the sweltering heat of the day this summer, Leo. Why don't you rest some of your regulars occasionally?" suggested veteran *Chicago Tribune* baseball writer Richard Dozer.

Durocher, an old-school baseball lifer if there ever was one, bristled at the notion. There were no lights for night games at Wrigley Field before 1988, but Durocher never would use the summer heat as an excuse for losing ballgames. He leaped from the chair in his cramped office before that day's scheduled game against the Cincinnati Reds. Standing at the top of the steps in the dank old clubhouse situated down the left-field line at Wrigley Field, Durocher motioned for Dozer to follow him into the locker room where all of us players were putting on our uniforms.

"Does anybody want to come out of the lineup because you are tired?" Durocher shouted.

None of us said a word.

"Beckert!" Durocher then yelled at our dependable second baseman. "Are you tired?"

"Nope," Beckert replied.

"How about you, Kessinger. Is the heat getting to you? Are you tired?" growled Durocher.

Don Kessinger, a slick-fielding shortstop, paused, then shrugged his shoulders before answering without looking up. "No, Leo. I'm not tired."

One by one, each of our starters told Durocher exactly what he wanted to hear as he turned and sneered at Dozer for the writer's audacity to challenge his strategy. There were about nine writers and sports columnists covering the Cubs in those days, including the highly critical *Chicago Today* columnist Rick Talley, who refused to ever refer to Durocher by name. He would always say, "Oh what's his name" when he was talking about Durocher.

Meanwhile, Leo would always say, "All of those nine guys are trying to get rid of me. They want me out of town." There was a lot of friction going on between Durocher and the Chicago media at the time.

Despite all of Durocher's denials, the results on the field the final month and a half of that bittersweet season told another story.

I think some of our guys counted their eggs before they were hatched.

Entering the 2007 season, the Cubs hadn't been to the World Series since 1945. They failed to make the playoffs between 1945 and 1984, a period of 39 years. The Cubs did manage to earn playoff berths in 1984, 1989, 1998, and 2003. They won a playoff round (against Atlanta) for the first time in more than 50 years in 2003, only to fail to make it to the World Series because of a collapse with just five outs to go in Game 6. That horrific loss came to be known as the "Bartman Game" because a fan named Steve Bartman reached over to catch a foul ball and distracted Cubs left fielder Moises Alou. I think it is blatantly unfair to pin that loss on a fan who was just simply trying to catch a fly ball that was coming toward him. The fact is, a subsequent error by shortstop Alex Gonzalez and the ineffectiveness of pitcher Mark Prior after that foul ball caused the loss in Game 6. And then the Florida Marlins went on to win Game 7 in that NL Championship Series.

You couldn't separate the fans from me, Ernie, Santo, and Leo, because we had some great years in Chicago.

But the disappointment of the 1969 season still seems to resonate the most with Cubs fans. After all, the last time the Cubs won a World Series was 1908.

Ernie Banks hit .253 with 23 homers and 106 RBIs in 1969, very respectable numbers, yet a shade below his Hall of Fame standards. But let's face it, Ernie was 38 years old in '69, and he played in 155 games. Amazing!

A favorite management tactic of Durocher was to sort of criticize one of the team leaders, just to let everyone know that he was in charge. Durocher seemed to do that with Banks, perhaps the franchise's most beloved player. Ernie's sunny disposition probably made him an easier target for Durocher, knowing that Banks would not react publicly in a negative way. But all of us players on the team knew what was going on.

In 1966, when Leo first came to the Cubs in spring training, he had a meeting with the ballclub. P.K. Wrigley, our owner, had given him *carte blanche* and he could do anything that he wanted. Leo was the man and he was going to run the club and do anything he could to get us into first place.

It wasn't from lack of trying that we failed. We just went into a collective slump at the wrong time.

On the first day of spring training, Leo jumped on our longtime clubhouse man, Yosh Kawano, for not having certain things ready for the players in the clubhouse. Leo said, "Anything the players want, I want you to set it up in the clubhouse for them. Do you understand, Yosh?"

Then Leo started in on Ernie. Durocher had helped broadcast some games on NBC before becoming our manager, and he noticed that when Fergie Jenkins or another one of our pitchers threw the ball over to Ernie at first base to keep the runner close, Ernie would throw the ball right back to the pitcher without trying to tag the runner.

Leo told Ernie, "Dammit, when the pitcher throws the ball to you, I don't want you to throw it right back to the pitcher. I want you to tag the runner at first. I don't give a shit if he is standing on the base or not."

Then Leo got on Ernie about not taking a big enough lead when he was on first base as a runner, even when there was a right-handed pitcher on the mound.

I could see where Leo was going by getting on the two senior people with the Cubs organization on the very first day of spring training. Later on I said to Leo, "You did that for a reason, didn't you?" He just looked at me and laughed. He never did acknowledge what was going on. But I knew. He got on the two senior guys right away. Leo just wanted everyone to know that he was the guy in charge. He was going to be the show. Leo had some great years around Chicago and the fans loved him. You couldn't separate the fans from me, Ernie, Santo, and Leo, because we had some great years in Chicago.

I remember telling a *Chicago Today* sportswriter, Jim Enright, about how Ernie wasn't getting to start all the time at first base early in the season. I told Enright, "Ernie has still got some juice left. Ernie can still help us win some games if he is in the lineup."

When my quotes showed up in the paper the next day, Mr. Wrigley called John Holland and Holland called Leo and told him I didn't like the way Ernie was being treated. We got it all resolved. That was Leo for you.

Adding to the exhilaration of being in a pennant race in 1969 was watching left-hander Ken Holtzman pitch a no-hitter. Kenny had made the leap from Class AA in the minors to the big leagues in 1965. He also had a National Guard military obligation in 1969 that saw him coming back and forth to our ballclub. I remember seeing him often show up at the ballpark wearing his military uniform.

Holtzman tossed a 3–0 no-hitter against the Atlanta Braves on August 19, 1969. He pitched a second no-hitter for the Cubs, defeating the Cincinnati Reds 1–0 on June 3, 1971. Holtzman scored the only run of that game.

His first no-hitter came while we were still enjoying being in first place in 1969, as standing-room-only crowds of 40,000 routinely packed the ballpark. We were 18–11 in the month of August.

The Braves' Hank Aaron hit a ball off Holtzman that appeared destined for the left-field bleachers in the seventh inning. I just knew it was gone for a homer, but the wind blew it back in and I was able to catch it up against the vines to preserve the no-hitter.

Holtzman was later quoted as saying, "A no-hit game is a well-pitched game with an added dose of luck." Holtzman was able to no-hit Atlanta despite failing to strike out a single batter.

On August 13, 1969, we held a 10-game lead over the New York Mets. Two weeks later, the lead was down to two-and-a-half games. We would then lose eight in a row in September while the Mets won 10 in a row.

After we fell out of first place, Leo got really frustrated and we had a 45-minute team meeting. He wanted us to take more batting practice. But that didn't seem to help as a lot of our players became increasingly frustrated as well. It wasn't from lack of trying that we failed. We just went into a collective slump at the wrong time.

In that meeting, we stayed in the clubhouse a long time. It started out with Leo saying, "Just look at me as a ballplayer today, not as a manager."

The main reason for the meeting was that we were on a long losing streak. It had leaked out that Ron Santo wanted a special ceremonial day for himself.

Leo pulled off his shirt and threw it on the floor of the clubhouse for added effect to start the meeting. He said, "You guys are a bunch of goddamn crybabies!"

They had a special day for Ernie, and the Cubs gave me a special day. Ronnie, who was a nine-time All-Star third baseman and a terrific fielder, didn't want to sign a new contract until he was guaranteed a special day for himself in Chicago. When Leo heard about that and confronted Ronnie in our team meeting, Ronnie's face got as red as a piece of beef. The two of them really started going at it. Ronnie chased Leo all the way up to where the manager's office is located in the clubhouse at Wrigley Field. Ronnie grabbed at Leo across the desk and we had to pull him back. Ronnie had chased him up there and he was going to strangle him.

Maybe we kept our eyes on the scoreboard more than on our playing field, and that surely took its toll.

There must have been a conversation between Leo and general manager John Holland that allowed Leo to find out that Ronnie wanted a special day.

Leo then threatened to leave the ballclub. Kenny Holtzman was in the corner of the clubhouse yelling, "Let him go, let him go!"

Then another player stood up and said, "We will be known as the crybabies of the league if we don't get things together." At that point, somebody called Holland and he came down from his office to the clubhouse to see what was going on in the meeting. There was a big mess in the clubhouse.

That team meeting lasted so long that we didn't come out on the field until about 20 minutes before the game started. But later that day, Ronnie went 4-for-4 at the plate. He was fired up.

In the end—the very bitter end—we finished eight games out of first place in 1969.

We weren't hitting well, we weren't pitching well, and we weren't fielding well. Did we get tired in the final two months of the season? I don't know. Maybe I was, but my production didn't reflect it. I felt like I was hitting okay at the end. I hit .278 in the month of September, with six home runs, and I finished the year batting .293 with 21 homers and 95 RBIs. It wasn't my best season, but it was not too shabby.

Frank Sinatra would always tell Leo that one day he would love to sit in the dugout and manage a Major League Baseball team.

If I had gone into a slump in that part of the season, I would have gone into the clubhouse and said to myself, What could I have done to help the ballclub win? But I left it all on the field. It wasn't my best, most productive year. But it was a good, solid year and I scored 103 runs. I already felt bad that we didn't win in '69, but I felt I did a decent job myself.

From 1961–1973 I opened every season batting third in the Cubs' lineup. In 1974, manager Whitey Lockman broke that streak when he inserted me in the cleanup slot on Opening Day.

Most of the years that I played, I weighed about 173 pounds on my 6'2" frame. Pretty skinny. During the dog days of 1969, a lot of the other guys tailed off. Randy Hundley, our catcher, would always lose so much weight during the course of a season. He caught 151 games that year. By September, Randy would need suspenders to hold his pants up because he had lost so much weight. We would stand behind him going up the stairs and pull on his suspenders and snap them, just for fun. We also snapped his suspenders on the plane when he walked down the aisle.

But going through the final month and a half of the '69 season certainly was no fun. Until the day I go to my grave, I will always say that the Mets won the division that year. We didn't lose it. They just played lights-out with great pitching from Tom Seaver, Jerry Koosman, Nolan Ryan, and Gary Gentry, and timely hitting from Cleon Jones, Tommie Agee, Donn Clendenon, Ed Kranepool, and Ron Swoboda.

The Mets were an expansion team that entered the National League in 1962. The Mets had not finished higher than ninth place prior to 1969, so you can imagine why few people took them seriously.

But that year just proved the old axiom that pitching and defense can win games for a team on a consistent basis. The Mets' pitching staff wound up with a collective 2.99 earned run average, led by Seaver with a 25–7 record and 2.21 ERA, and Koosman at 17–9 and 2.28.

It was hard for me to watch the World Series that year. The Mets had advanced to the fall classic by sweeping the Atlanta Braves before taking four of five games in the World Series against the shocked Baltimore Orioles.

As our slide continued late in the season and the Mets continued to win, I did my best to try to encourage my teammates. There were eight small mirrors on the wall in our old Wrigley Field clubhouse. In fact, there were more mirrors than showers for the whole team. Each day I would take a bar of soap and write "$23,000" on the mirrors. That's how much more money each of us could make if we would win the World Series in 1969. Not a bad postseason paycheck back in those days.

But it seemed like the harder we tried, the more we failed. Even if we were to win two out of three in a series, the Mets would win three out of three in their series. Maybe we kept our eyes on the scoreboard more than on our playing field, and that surely took its toll.

Cubs fans never lost faith, not until the very end when we were mathematically eliminated. They didn't boo us, they always thought we could come back and overtake the Mets. Especially the Mets.

The fans won't let us forget. They will keep in their memory banks the joy that they had.

Everything had been set up for us to win it all in 1969, or so it seemed. We had played a lot of basketball during that winter to stay in shape as a team. We were determined to be ready for the '69 baseball season.

The foundation for the '69 season began the previous year. Our starting lineup was pretty much set: Banks at first, Glenn Beckert at second, Don Kessinger at short, and Ron Santo at third. Hundley was the catcher, Jim Hickman was in right field, and I was in left. The only position that was a bit unsettled was center field, where Adolfo Phillips began the year before Don Young took over. Jim Qualls, Al Spangler, and Oscar Gamble also gave it a shot in center field that year.

Phillips seemed to have the talent to become a superstar in the majors. I recall seeing him hit four homers in a double-header and everyone called him the "Panamanian Flash." But after that he was knocked down with a pitch and he was never the same player afterwards.

Most of us had played together for so long and got along so well both on and off the field.

On June 11, 1969, we received infielder Paul Popovich from the Montreal Expos in exchange for Phillips and pitcher Jack Lamabe. Adolfo was a popular player on our team then. He shook hands with everyone while leaving, except Durocher.

Kessinger started 20 of the last 25 games in September of '69, and Popovich started the other five contests. Popovich had previously filled in nicely for the injured Beckert at second base in the month of June.

Our pitching staff included future Hall of Famer Fergie Jenkins, Holtzman, Bill Hands, and Dick Selma as starters. Jenkins (21–15) and Hands (20–14) were our two 20-game winners and Holtzman won 17 games.

In the bullpen, Phil Regan, known as "The Vulture," appeared in 71 games and had a 12–6 record and 17 saves. Ted Abernathy also was a major contributor out of the bullpen with his submarine pitching style, along with Hank Aguirre and Rich Nye. Durocher also caught a lot of flak for overusing Regan because he became less effective late in the season.

We appeared pretty solid at every position and a lot of the media had predicted the Cubs to win it all before the '69 season started. In the spring of that year the focus was for all of us to have fun and be in top physical shape.

We played cards together during our free time, went out to dinner together, and maintained an attitude of cohesion. Even our wives and other family members often socialized together.

The atmosphere was always positive in spring training, even though Durocher was generally intense and serious. Durocher always hung around with the Hollywood types and they loved being around him, especially that spring.

I remember one spring training game we had in Palm Springs, California. Frank Sinatra would always tell Leo that one day he would love to sit in the dugout and manage a Major League Baseball team. Well, Durocher finally gave him his chance that spring training and he had a blast. At one point late in that game, Sinatra became confused about what managerial move to make. "Old Blue Eyes" stuck his head out of the dugout and said, "What do I do now, Leo?"

Durocher just looked at him, shook his head, and laughed. "You are the one who wanted to be the manager," he said.

Durocher had become our manager on October 25, 1965, replacing Lou Klein (48–58), who was the head of the failed "College of Coaches" experiment for the Cubs in 1961 and '62.

> But it seemed that all of that stuff that happened in 1968—the rioting in Chicago, and all of the other social unrest here—a lot of that was behind us by spring training of 1969.

We used our regular coaching staff in '61 and '62 with a rotating system of managers—the College of Coaches—that included Vedie Himsl, Harry Craft, Elvin Tappe, Charlie Metro, and Klein. The innovative idea of owner P.K. Wrigley didn't work out very well. We were 64–90 in 1961 and 59–103 in 1962. Bob Kennedy took over as manager in '63.

Durocher was a colorful character, to put it politely. He was often brash, irascible, and demanding. He was involved in baseball for nearly five decades as a player, manager, coach, and television commentator.

He spent his first full major league season as a player with the 1928 world champion Yankees. Durocher became New York's starting shortstop in 1929. He was traded to the Reds in 1930, and the Cardinals in 1933. That is where he became captain of the famed "Gas House Gang" in 1934.

Durocher was a light-hitting shortstop during his 17-year playing career, but he was respected for his fielding and scrappy play.

He became a player-manager for the Dodgers in 1939, guiding the Dodgers to the NL pennant in 1941 and to second-place finishes in 1940, 1942, and 1946.

In spring training of 1947, Durocher ended a rebellion of Dodgers players who protested the presence of Jackie Robinson as the first black player in Major League Baseball.

Leo definitely loved the fast life, spending plenty of time at the racetrack and at Hollywood parties. He was indicted in 1945 for assaulting a fan under the stands. Then, in 1947, he was suspended for the season for his alleged association with gamblers. The Dodgers won the pennant that year with Burt Shotton taking over for Durocher. Leo moved on to the New York Giants and won two pennants and the World Series in 1954.

As the 1969 season approached, most of us focused our attention on the St. Louis Cardinals as our number one competitor. The Cardinals had a veteran team with stars such as Lou Brock, Bob Gibson, and Joe Torre. You always knew they would be tough to beat. None of us thought about the Mets, an expansion team managed then by Gil Hodges.

Our first game set the tone for an incredible first four-and-one-half months of the season. The home opener is always so exciting anyway.

Pat Pieper, who introduced the starting lineups to the fans in Wrigley Field, would always begin by saying, "Attention! Attention, please! Get your pencils and scorecards ready and I will give you the correct lineup for today's ballgame."

Pieper was a fixture at Wrigley Field from 1916 to 1974. I was told that he used a megaphone to announce the line-ups until a public address system was installed in 1931.

Well, in the home opener in 1969, we were in a tie ball-game with the Phillies. Philadelphia scored three runs in the top of the ninth to tie the game 5–5. In the top of the eleventh, the Phillies took a 6–5 lead. Then, in the bottom of the eleventh, with one out and a man on base, pinch-hitter Willie Smith stepped to the plate. He blasted a home run into the right-field bleachers to win the game 7–6.

Wrigley Field erupted as fans became hysterical. And so did we as Cubs players.

I had a special fondness for Willie Smith because he was another Alabama kid. He was from Anniston, Alabama. Nicknamed "Wonderful Willie," he had broken into the big leagues with the Detroit Tigers in 1963 and also played for the Angels, Indians, and Reds, and he had a reputation as a terrific left-handed clutch hitter. I was saddened to hear that he died at the age of 66 on January 16, 2006, in Anniston.

We knew, somehow, that we were going to win that open-ing game. We just didn't know it was going to be Willie Smith. When he hit the ball out of the ballpark, the fans went crazy. The timing of his big hit could not have been better. That home run was just the start of what was going to happen to us.

We won 11 of our first 12 games and, man, were we hav-ing fun doing it. We would not fall out of first place for 155 days. The fans were loving it and our most die-hard fans—

the Bleacher Bums—became an integral part of the scene at Wrigley Field. We were treated like rock stars, signing autographs and posing for pictures everywhere we went. Back in those days, the players' parking lot was located across Waveland Avenue where the fire station is now located beyond the left-field fence. So many fans would be waiting for us after the game for autographs that we had to literally run to our cars. But it was such a fun time in my life. The games were being televised on WGN-TV and the Cubs were a good partner for them. Everybody was able to see the Cubs all over the country.

On May 13, 1969, Ernie Banks had seven RBIs, including his 1,500th on a three-run homer during a 19–0 blowout of San Diego. It matched the biggest shutout margin in major league history. Dick Selma earned the victory with his three-hit pitching performance. We had obtained Selma from the Padres earlier in the season. It was the third straight shutout thrown by our pitchers. Fergie Jenkins and Ken Holtzman managed this feat before Selma's great performance.

After every victory at home, Santo would jump up in the air and click his heels on the way to the clubhouse. I know a lot of the guys on other teams in the league didn't like that. They thought maybe he was rubbing it in a little bit. But Ronnie was just jubilant and happy that we won a game in front of our faithful fans.

When I woke up each morning I couldn't wait to get to the ballpark. We expected to win every day. I owned a Buick Wildcat during the summer of '69. As I drove around Chicago, fans would wave and flash me a peace sign. I think it would be impossible to try to recreate that feeling we had in Chicago in '69.

As Cubs players in 1969, there was no barrier between us and the fans. When we went across the street to get in our cars after games, we had to sign autographs. There was no fence, there was nothing. And we always got a kick out of being with the fans. And they got a kick out of being with us. It is good to see that after 40 years, people still come up and remember 1969, just like it was yesterday. The fans won't let us forget. They will keep in their memory banks the joy that they had. I think they have scratched out the last month from their minds. They had more fun than sadness, so they just eliminated the bad part. They are living with three-quarters of the '69 season.

I attended a special ceremony this year and an individual came up to me. He said that in 1969 he was in the streets, getting into trouble, doing all kinds of stuff. And the guy told me that he heard me on the radio being interviewed that year and I said some things that kind of turned his life around. Then he started crying. That is the kind of gratification I got from that year. That is what you want to hear.

The late 1960s represented some turbulent times in America, and especially Chicago, where race riots and political demonstrations were the norm. It seemed as if a lot of people needed to get away and let off some steam by going to the ballpark. Even today, I run into people who are 50 or 60 years old who tell me, "Thank you for the joy that you brought me during that '69 season." That really makes me feel special and proud.

The 1968 Democratic Convention was held in Chicago, and the social and political unrest at the time sparked riots and chaos both locally and across the country as different factions protested the Vietnam War.

It was on April 4, 1968, when Rev. Martin Luther King Jr. was assassinated in Memphis, Tennessee. That set off riots in more than 100 cities across America, including Chicago. Nine blacks were killed and 20 blocks were set ablaze in Chicago immediately after his assassination.

About a week later, then-President Lyndon Johnson signed the Civil Rights Act of 1968, which was supposed to address the issue of open housing in America. And then a few days later, Chicago Mayor Richard J. Daley criticized the police chief for not being more aggressive with protestors who were rioting after the assassination of Dr. King. Daley sent out the order "to shoot to kill any arsonist or anyone with a Molotov cocktail in his hand, because they're potential murderers, and to shoot to maim or cripple anyone looting."

In the spring of 1968, we were playing an exhibition game in Lafayette, Indiana. We checked into the hotel and a bunch of us said that we were going to meet and go down for dinner. The assassination of Dr. King hit so many people so hard. Lou Johnson, who is black, started to step into the elevator. When the elevator opened up, Randy Hundley, who is white, was standing there. At that point, Lou refused to get in the elevator because of the anger he was feeling at that time. It was nothing personal against Hundley. Lou was just so angry at what had happened. That assassination brought a lot of hatred out of a lot of people.

Later that same year, on June 5, Senator Robert Kennedy was assassinated in Los Angeles immediately after declaring victory in the California Democratic primary.

So it was amid that backdrop that baseball fans sought refuge from the daily pressures of war, politics, and community violence.

But it seemed that all of that stuff that happened in 1968—the rioting in Chicago, and all of the other social unrest here—a lot of that was behind us by spring training of 1969. Going into the 1969 season we were ready to roll over everybody. As a matter of fact, we weren't thinking about the Mets. We were thinking about the Cardinals.

On the field in '69 we seemed to maintain our focus for the first five months of the season.

On June 15, 1969, Kessinger set a National League record with his 54th straight errorless game to start the season. But we dropped a 7–6 decision in the first game of a doubleheader in Cincinnati.

One of the biggest highlights of my career occurred on June 29, 1969. That was the day I broke Stan Musial's streak for consecutive games played by a National Leaguer. Stan "The Man" Musial, as he was known, is a Hall of Famer from the St. Louis Cardinals and regarded as one of the top ballplayers of all time. That day was especially exciting for me because the Cubs had declared it Billy Williams Day at Wrigley Field—and we were playing the Cardinals in a doubleheader! We swept the Cardinals 3–1 and 12–1 in front of 41,060 fans.

Two weeks before, in Cincinnati, I hit a foul ball off my foot and I feared it was broken. Luckily, it was just badly bruised and we had a day off before my special day at Wrigley.

In the first game of the doubleheader, I got a hit to help us win 3–1.

Between games, a special ceremony was held to commemorate my record for consecutive games played. That streak would extend to 1,117 games played. My mother came up for the game from our home in Whistler, Alabama. My aunt came up too. The stands were packed and I was later told that some 10,000 people who wanted to get in the ballpark were turned away. I told my mother before the game started, "Now, Mom. You know there are going to be a lot of people at the ballpark when you stand out there on the field. So don't you go fainting on me." She just laughed.

During the ceremony they showered me with so many gifts. I was given a boat and a lounge chair. And the club spared no expense by giving me a brown Chrysler Imperial with a black top. Ron Santo had a friend in the jewelry business who had a necklace made for my wife. Shirley wears that necklace with my No. 26 on it to this day and loves telling the story about how she got it. All in all, it was a beautiful ceremony, one I will never forget.

But the second game of that doubleheader against the Cardinals would bring more fireworks. Most importantly, we won the game 12–1. Secondly, I went 4-for-5 at the plate, including a single, a double, and two triples. When I came to the plate for my last at-bat, needing a home run to hit for the cycle on Billy Williams Day, the fans stood and cheered. I tried so hard to hit a home run, probably too hard. I wound up striking out. But as I was walking to the dugout with my head down, the fans just continued to cheer to show their appreciation for me. I got really emotional after hearing that ovation, and the memory still gives me goose pimples.

What a terrific day that was for me. And to top it off, that was the day we moved eight-and-a-half games ahead into first place.

On July 14, we edged the Mets 1–0 behind Bill Hands's win against Tom Seaver. I singled home the game-winner to give us a five–and–one-half game lead over the Mets. At the end of that game, Santo infuriated the Mets by jumping up and clicking his heels in glee.

By August 27, our lead over the Mets had slipped to two-and-a-half games. A 6–3 loss to the Reds was our seventh in our last nine games.

One of the most symbolic memories that sort of represented our frustration as a team in 1969 was Hundley hopping up and down at home plate following a disputed call against the Mets in New York's Shea Stadium on September 8.

Hands was our pitcher and his first pitch of the ballgame knocked Tommie Agee on his butt. That signaled how contentious this ballgame and rivalry would become.

Agee climbed to his feet, brushed himself off, and proceeded to crack a slider over the center-field wall for a homer.

Jerry Koosman would retaliate for the Mets by knocking down Santo with a pitch.

The most controversial play involved a two-out at-bat by the Mets' Wayne Garrett with the score tied 2–2. He rapped a hit to right field and Jim Hickman made a great throw to the plate that was up the third-base line a little bit. Hundley caught the throw and tagged Agee "from his thighs all the way up to his chin almost," as Hundley recalls.

But umpire Satch Davidson called Agee safe. The Mets won the game 3–2, and we remained mired in an eight-game losing streak.

Hundley, who continues to host his Fantasy Baseball Camp in Arizona every spring, still talks about that play against the Mets to this day. "The way that I had to swipe at him, the umpire evidently thought that I had missed him. But I had tagged him so hard that I almost dropped the ball," Hundley says. "The ball went up in the webbing of my mitt and I was able to hold on. Whenever you see the replay, you realize that players are not actors. If I had missed the tag, what's the first thing I am going to do? I am going to go back and try to tag him.

"So I tagged Agee [the first time], and I turned around to make sure the runner didn't go to second base. [Garrett] saw me tag Agee and he is looking disgusted down at first. Then all of a sudden I hear this tremendous roar go up and I said, 'Oh, no, I can't believe this.'

"I turned and Satch Davidson has got the safe sign going down. I just went berserk. I knew I had to jump up and down in order to stay away and not make contact with him, or else I would be suspended.

"The Mets won that ballgame and it was a big swing game for us. I knew that right then and there that this was going to be a big play. I knew it was going to be a big play for the entire season. The Mets had to know that they did get a big break there."

One of the ugliest moments of that '69 season occurred when Don Young made two costly misplays in center field during a game against the Mets at Shea Stadium on July 8. Young was just a kid, 23 years old. When you are playing in Shea Stadium the sun is often right in your face as a center fielder. This particular day Fergie Jenkins was pitching for us.

A ball was hit to center and Young dropped it. I kept telling him all day to try to relax, but it was tough for a young kid. We lost that game and afterward Santo ripped into Young in a newspaper interview. Young was so upset that he didn't even ride on the team bus following the game. I saw Ronnie in the lobby of our hotel the next morning and

I told him, "Why don't you say something in the paper tomorrow to soften up this situation. Because this kid Don Young really has his confidence shaken."

Ron tried to do that the next day, but the damage had been done. When we got back to Chicago a lot of the fans at Wrigley Field booed Ronnie because of what he had said. Over the years, Young has pretty much gone into hibernation, even though it has been 38 years since he dropped that ball in the sun. Young batted .239 for us in 1969, which would be his last year in the big leagues.

We wanted Young to know that he will always be one of our teammates. We are like family.

I really feel bad for Young. For years he would not show up for any of our '69 Cubs reunions. The first year Randy Hundley started his Fantasy Baseball Camps down in Arizona, he invited Young to join us. Young showed up but he was too embarrassed to come into the clubhouse with his former teammates. Finally, Beckert and Kessinger physically escorted him into the clubhouse. It was quite an emotional moment. We wanted Young to know that he will always be one of our teammates. We are like family.

We dropped to second place on September 10 after losing to the Phillies 6–2. Meanwhile, the Mets swept the Montreal Expos, 3–2 and 7–1, to take a one-game lead in the division.

We continued to swoon and wound up with a 8–17 record in the month of September. Our final record was 92–70. The Mets took the NL pennant with a record of 100–62.

In looking back at that '69 season, it was one of the strangest and most inexplicable things in baseball. The fans had a lot of fun. Had we won the World Series in 1969, I truly believe we would have won one or two more. That's how talented that team was. We just couldn't get over the hump.

It seems like every other day you think about it because you were in that position to win. I often ask myself, "What if we had been there in the World Series?" It would have solved the question of what kind of player I would have been in the World Series, because I never got a chance to do it. Ernie Banks never got a chance to do it. If we had won the pennant that particular year...that still lingers in my mind. It gets to me. I think about it a lot because we were in a perfect spot to do it all year. That following winter I thought about it a lot. But as time goes by you have to forget about these things and go on with your life. I know that you cannot redirect the past. You just have to look to the future.

Had we won the World Series in 1969, I truly believe we would have won one or two more.

There would have been a big celebration in Chicago if we had won in 1969 because of the fans of that era and the players we had on that ballclub. I think we knew everybody who came to the ballpark by name back in those days because in the early '60s there would only be 5,000 or 6,000 people at the ballpark. By 1969 the Bleacher Bums started filling the ballpark. Most of us players had been together for so many years. It would have been a great feeling to compete in and win a World Series. Although we didn't win, I think one of the gratifying things was the fact that the fans in Chicago and all over the world have told me that 1969 was the greatest year they have experienced for the Cubs in Wrigley Field.

Even though I was blessed to be selected for the Hall of Fame in 1987, I often wonder how my baseball legacy might have changed if we had won the World Series in 1969. After all, fans associate Reggie Jackson with hitting three home runs in a World Series game against the Dodgers. He is known to this day as "Mr. October." I would have loved to have been on that national stage to see how I might have responded.

It does make me feel proud today, however, knowing that the '69 season was the beginning of the hysteria surrounding today's Cubs teams.

It does make me feel proud today, however, knowing that the '69 season was the beginning of the hysteria surrounding today's Cubs teams. Before Durocher became our manager in the 1966 season, the crowds at Wrigley Field were routinely sparse. Nowadays, it is difficult to get a ticket to a Cubs home game.

I still say that we didn't lose the pennant in 1969. Those damn Mets just wouldn't lose.

CHAPTER 3

The Mobile Mafia

Folks back in Mobile, Alabama, and the surrounding area like to joke around and say there must be something in the water down there that produces so many outstanding major league ballplayers.

Hank Aaron, Satchel Paige, Willie McCovey, Ozzie Smith, and many others came from around there. Willie Mays was actually born in Westfield, Alabama, just outside of Birmingham, but we like to claim him too. I felt blessed to join that elite group as a fellow Hall of Famer in 1987. Other contemporaries of mine who made it in the big leagues included Tommie Aaron, Amos Otis, Tommie Agee, Milt Bolling, Frank Bolling, Cleon Jones, and Buddy Bradford.

At one time the New York Mets had three guys in their outfield from Mobile—Agee, Jones, and Otis. That's kind of unusual. We are all proud of that. We all went off to play baseball and we wanted to be the best ballplayers up in the big leagues. We proved it over the years with the home runs, the MVP awards, and the Rookie of the Year awards. In fact, Willie McCovey, Tommie Agee, and I were all Rookies of the Year at one time.

I think we are also very proud that all of us who made it in the big leagues turned out to be good, solid citizens as well. When each of us made an impact in the major leagues as players, I think we all felt as if we were representing the Mobile area.

My former high school civics teacher in Whistler was Mrs. Valena McCants, who also served as a surrogate mother to all of the children of Whistler.

She used to step on my shined shoes or do whatever she had to do in those days to get us to respond. You can't do that sort of thing anymore. But she would also walk home with the students on occasion. That wasn't uncommon. That's the kind of upbringing we had. It was a common practice of all the teachers to kind of see their pupils as their kids. That is how it was.

My high school football coach, Virgil Rhodes, once paddled me when I was a youngster. Actually, he put the wood to me a couple of times. I thanked him for it later. I was by no means a troublemaker, but I guess I stepped beyond my bounds several times. That was the kind of discipline we all became accustomed to over the years because the adults cared about us.

My late father was Frank "Susie" Williams, who was a railroad worker and a right-handed hitting first baseman. He also had a sweet swing, and that is what earned him his unusual nickname in amateur baseball circles in Alabama. He tried to teach me to play third base when I was a kid because I was so tall. But playing the outfield worked out pretty well for me.

My birthplace remains a welcome throwback to a simpler life where baseball and family values seem to go hand in hand. I am one of five children. My mother was a very supportive parent and I think that's where my strength came from. We were a big, humble family.

I remember playing marbles in the yard of our neighbor, Mrs. Carrie Turner. Those were some competitive matches, full of the same tension and fervor of an extra-inning baseball game.

I am a couple of years older than my wife, Shirley. The teachers always would try to keep us separated when we were in school because I was a little older. Well, you see how that worked out. We have four lovely daughters now.

Ozzie Smith became the fifth native of Mobile added to the National Baseball Hall of Fame in 2002, joining Hank Aaron, McCovey, Paige, and me. Actually, Paige was selected through a special Veterans Committee vote. I have since learned that only four cities— Chicago, Brooklyn, New York, and San Francisco—have produced more baseball Hall of Famers than Mobile. Chicago has produced seven: Charles Comiskey, Jocko Conlon, Billy Evans, Will Harridge, Freddie Lindstrom, Kirby Puckett, and Bill Veeck.

When each of us made an impact in the major leagues as players, I think we all felt as if we were representing the Mobile area.

Brooklyn claims five Hall of Famers: Waite Hoyt, Willie Keeler, Sandy Koufax, Phil Rizzuto, and Mickey Welch.

New York City also takes credit for five: Alexander Cartwright, Whitey Ford, Lou Gehrig, Hank Greenberg, and George Wright.

San Francisco matches Mobile with four Hall of Famers: Joe Cronin, Harry Heilmann, Tony Lazzeri, and George Kelly.

When it comes to the states with the most Hall of Famers, Alabama has 11. Only six states have produced more: New

York (27), Illinois (19), Pennsylvania (19), Ohio (17), California (16), and Texas (13).

In addition to Aaron, Paige, McCovey, Mays, Smith, and me, other Alabama natives in the Hall of Fame are Monte Irvin, Heinie Manush, Joe Sewell, Don Sutton, and Early Wynn.

Aaron, McCovey, and Smith were first-ballot Hall of Famers.

> **My birthplace remains a welcome throwback to a simpler life where baseball and family values seem to go hand in hand.**

Irvin often is overlooked as a tremendous player who had to endure extreme racism after making the leap from the Negro Leagues to the big leagues. He played eight seasons in the big leagues, seven with the New York Giants and his last with the Cubs in 1956. Irvin was born in a small town called Haleburg, Alabama. He could do it all: run, hit, hit for power, and field. He was a tremendous model for all of us to follow in the big leagues as a player and a man of character. He was inducted into the Hall of Fame in 1973 and later served in the Office of the Commissioner of Baseball as a public relations specialist.

Now Tommie Aaron was no Hall of Famer, but he was an awfully good baseball player. I think that if he had been with another ballclub other than the Braves, he would have gotten more playing time. He was a good first baseman and he could play all the other infield positions, as well as the outfield. And Tommie could hit. It was just tough for him to be on the Atlanta Braves with his older brother being Hank Aaron. And it really hurt Hank when

Tommie passed away in 1984 at the age of 45. That tore him up.

Tommie went to Central High and I went to Mobile Training School; we used to play football against each other in the annual Thanksgiving Day match-ups.

As amateur baseball players, we never did play against the white teams in the Mobile area at that time. We would travel to places like New Orleans or Biloxi, Mississippi, or other small towns in Alabama to face other all-black teams. That was some good baseball at the time. But I could tell the difference between playing semi-pro baseball and playing professional baseball, in terms of the quality of play. You had the great coaches in professional ball.

I remember there was an amateur player named Allan Wolf, who was a pretty good pitcher in Mobile. I know he was trying to make a name for himself when he faced me, so I wound up hitting one over the right-field fence and one over the left-field fence against him.

I also recall going to Mitchell Field in Mobile to watch Henry Aaron play. That's what folks from Mobile always call him: "Henry." It wasn't until he got to the big leagues before some people began calling him "Hank."

Of course, I was down there with my older brother, Clyde, who was a left-handed pitcher. He played on the same team— the Mobile Black Bears—with Hank. At the time Aaron played second base; he hadn't shifted to the outfield yet. He was a cross-handed-hitting second baseman, but he hit line drives all over the place.

There was a man named Ed Tucker in Mobile and if there was any kid in Mobile who wanted to play baseball, he was the one who made sure you got the chance by putting you on his ballclub. Aaron played a couple of years of semi-pro ball, then, before you knew it, the Indianapolis Clowns of the Negro Leagues signed him. At that time the Indianapolis Clowns were similar to the Harlem Globetrotters in basketball. There was a lot of showmanship and they traveled all over the country. They would go through a phantom infield routine where they pretended to throw the ball around, the same way the Globetrotters pretended to pass a basketball around in a circle on the court.

We would travel to places like New Orleans or Biloxi, Mississippi, or other small towns in Alabama to face other all-black teams.

A woman named Toni Stone was a terrific player, but she was not allowed to play in the "whites only" All-American Girls Professional Baseball League that was popularized in the movie *A League of Their Own*. That's why she had to play on the all-male Indianapolis Clowns.

When Aaron later signed with the Boston Braves, Stone played second base for the Indianapolis Clowns. In 1954 Stone played for the Kansas City Monarchs. She wound up with a respectable career batting average of .240, and she could turn the double play at second base as well as anyone.

Toward the end of her memorable and pioneering career, she had a chance to play with Satchel Paige with the Monarchs. Stone once said that Satch was so good, "that he'd ask batters where they wanted it, just so they'd have a chance. He'd ask, 'You want it high? You want it low? You want it right in the middle? Just say.' People still couldn't get a hit against him."

A scout named Ivy Griffin signed me to my first pro contract when I was only 17, just two days after I finished high school in 1956. I turned 18 a couple of weeks later. I got $1,500 to sign. That's when I reported here (second row) to Ponca City, Oklahoma.

Here I am with the Houston Buffs of the American Association.

I made my major league debut on August 6, 1959, as we beat the Phillies 4-2 that day. I hit .152 that year, getting only 33 at-bats. In 1960, I improved to .277 in 47 at-bats.

I was named NL Rookie of the Year in 1961. I hit 25 homers and drove in 86 runs in only 146 games while batting .278.

Ken Hubbs (left), Lindy McDaniel, and I joking around following a victory at Wrigley Field. In 1962, Hubbs was named NL Rookie of the Year, giving the Cubs the award two straight years.

When I first met Ernie Banks (right) in Mesa, Arizona, during spring training in 1958, I found him to be one of the most talented guys that you would ever want to meet.

My father, Frank Williams, was a well-known amateur ballplayer for the Whistler Stars, and some said he had the skills as a first baseman to play in the big leagues had the color barrier not existed in the 1920s and '30s.

My older brother, Franklin (center) and Buck O'Neil (right) were two of the most influential people in my life as a baseball player.

Shirley and I have been married since February 25, 1960. At least Shirley did not have to change her last name—her maiden name also was Williams.

Longtime Cubs announcer Jack Brickhouse truly loved the Cubs and we respected his knowledge of the game.

Here I am being presented a trophy on "Billy Williams Day" at Wrigley Field. The stands were packed that day, and I was later told that some 10,000 people were turned away from the ballpark.

My mother, Mary (left) and my aunt, Olivet Lewis flanked me on "Billy Williams Day."

My mother (Mary, left) came up for the "Billy Williams Day" game from our home in Whistler, Alabama. My aunt came up, as well.

Here are my girls—Nina, Julia, Sandy, and Valerie—in front of the Cubs dugout in full uniform on "Billy Williams Day," June 29, 1969.

I was overcome with emotion by the events of "Billy Williams Day."

Once in her career, Stone got a hit off of Paige and called it the happiest moment in her life.

Now Hank Aaron was always a steady player. When he first came up to the big leagues he did everything with ease. And some people pinned the handle on him that he was lazy and didn't go all out. But that was his temperament. He could run well and he was a smart base runner. He could throw with anybody, he could hit, and he always was consistent at the plate. When he first came into the league he really wasn't a pull hitter. He hit the ball all over the place and that is the way he was when I saw him grow up as a cross-handed-hitting infielder.

When I was with the Cubs in the early '60s, we would go up to Milwaukee to play the Braves at County Stadium. After the games, Hank and I would spend time together and have dinner or go other places for a cold one. When the Braves moved to Atlanta there would be three or four buses full of friends and fans from Mobile who would come down to see the games, especially when the Mets or Cubs were in town because both clubs had other players from Mobile on them. That's how the people of Mobile supported their athletes down there.

When I was playing in the minor leagues in the late 1950s, I used to keep up with Aaron. Then, after he played for a while, all of the current big leaguers who lived down in Mobile used to work out together before we went to spring training.

We had about 15 guys from the area who would get together regularly just before the start of spring training. For most of the off-season, we wouldn't do anything but bowl. None of us was very good at bowling. But that wasn't the point. We just wanted to do something physical, have fun, and enjoy the camaraderie. Then, about three weeks before spring training would start in Arizona or Florida, we would get serious. Nobody picked up a glove until then back in those days because we had to work another job. Then we would all meet up with Aaron in Thomasville, Alabama, where he lived. It would be Tommie Agee, Cleon Jones, Willie McCovey, Amos Otis, George Scott, Milt Bolling and Frank Bolling, my brother Franklin, and some others. Scott actually was from Mississippi.

Franklin signed with the Pittsburgh Pirates as an infielder/outfielder in 1955. He went off to Grand Forks, North Dakota, and his last years in pro ball were with the Pirates' Triple A club in Lincoln, Nebraska. I got him a try-out with the Cubs, but the Cubs wouldn't sign him because he had played Negro League baseball and the Cubs would have had to pay that league so much money in exchange. Franklin played in the last Negro League Baseball All-Star Game in 1960 at Comiskey Park in Chicago, which drew 50,000 fans.

Tommie Agee, Amos Otis, and Cleon Jones are among the last of the Mobile guys from my era who played in the major leagues. Buddy Bradford came along a little later and played 11 big-league seasons, mainly for the Chicago White Sox as an outfielder during the 1960s and '70s.

I played defensive end on the football team my senior year of high school and Agee took my position when I left there. And Cleon was a good running back in Mobile. Cleon wound up being signed by the New York Mets and Agee signed with the Indians and was the American League Rookie of the Year with the White Sox. Sam Hairston, the first black ballplayer for the White Sox, became a scout and signed Agee for $85,000.

When the group of us from the Mobile area would take batting practice during the off-season, we didn't have a protective screen in front of the pitcher like they do in the big leagues. But what we did was hit the ball to the opposite field for a while and then we would pull some balls. If the ball was inside, we would pull it. If it was outside, we would go to the opposite field. We made it a point that nobody hit a ball through the middle. We wouldn't swing at the ball right down the middle of the plate that we couldn't steer. Each of us took about two or three rounds of about 20 swings, then we would sit in the stands and just talk baseball.

Aaron was the senior member of our group at the time so he would tell us what to expect in the big leagues and how to go about our business in the major leagues. At the end of our three-week session of getting ready for spring training we would say to each other, "I will see you down the road."

Aaron's personality has not changed one bit throughout the many years. He was always soft-spoken and deliberate with everything he did. But he also possessed an indomitable will to succeed while overcoming obstacles such as racism right up until the time he broke Babe Ruth's hallowed career home-run record in 1974.

He found himself in an awkward position in 2007 as Barry Bonds approached his home-run record. With all of the controversy and speculation surrounding Bonds's alleged use of steroids to enhance his home-run power, Aaron was urged to give his hearty support to Bonds. A lot of people wondered why Aaron did not follow Bonds around the country for two weeks as he approached the mark. But let's face it, Aaron is 73 years old and it would not have been feasible for him to do that. In the end, I thought he handled the whole situation with class. He had taped a message of congratulations to Bonds that was shown when the record was broken in San Francisco. The message was shown on the video screen and it really seemed to touch Bonds, who became quite emotional.

Even after he stopped hitting cross-handed, Hank still had an unorthodox way of batting, but it worked well enough to make him the all-time home-run king until Bonds came along to break his record of 755.

When Hank came up to bat in the 1957 World Series against the Yankees, catcher Yogi Berra told him, "You have the brand of the bat facing the wrong way." Aaron turned to Berra and said, "I didn't come up here to read; I came up here to hit."

I had mixed emotions when I saw Bonds break Hank's home-run record on August 8, 2007.

I am kind of partial to Aaron, coming from the same hometown and remembering him from Mobile. I always said that records are made to be broken. And Barry came up as a good player. The accusations about the steroids...I don't know if he was taking them or when he was taking them. But he always has been a great ballplayer, winning seven Most Valuable Player awards. When he takes off his uniform for the last time, Bonds will be regarded as one of the greatest players who ever played. When you look at the home runs, the intentional walks, and all of the things he did over the years, he is a great ballplayer. And he was a Gold Glove outfielder in left field.

Barry is still swinging the bat really well at the age of 43. He is not lacking velocity of the bat through the strike zone. I think his home-run record is a great feat. No one thought this would happen. I thought Hank's record of 755 home runs was one that would stand for a long, long time. Right along with Joe DiMaggio's 56-game hitting streak and Cal Ripken's consecutive-games-played mark of 2,632.

The thing about Aaron is that he never hit 50 home runs in a single season. His best home-run year was when he hit 47 in 1971. But he showed consistency, hitting 40 or more homers in eight of his 23 seasons. Some people felt that Aaron sort of snuck up on Ruth's record because he did not have that one monster year like Bonds did when he hit 73 homers in 2001. Plus, the fact that Aaron always has been so modest and quiet, a lot of people overlooked what he was doing while some of the more outgoing and gregarious players were soaking in the spotlight.

Another important factor to be examined is that the pitching quality in the big leagues today has been diluted, compared to the era that Aaron and I played. With all of the expansion teams in baseball nowadays, there are a lot of pitchers with similar flaws who would be in the minor league system during the 1950s, '60s, and '70s. The good hitters of today, like Bonds and Ken Griffey Jr., have had a field day for the last 15 years. When I played, the pitching mound was higher and it was the era of the pitcher.

Between the 1968 and '69 season, the Playing Rules Committee decided to lower the height of the pitching mound from 15 inches to 10 inches. The new ruling also stipulated that the mounds be sloped in order to reduce the angle pitchers had on us hitters. Unfortunately for me, I was toward my latter years in the big leagues and could not take full advantage of the new rule. Clearly, the pitchers had the advantage prior to the '69 season.

Try facing Bob Gibson, Juan Marichal, Don Drysdale, Warren Spahn, or Sandy Koufax from a 15-inch mound that is not sloped. They were throwing bullets downhill while we were trying to catch up with them with our bats.

> **If the ball was inside, we would pull it. If it was outside, we would go to the opposite field. We made it a point that nobody hit a ball through the middle.**

Breaking Aaron's record is a great feat, don't get me wrong. But a lot of things have to go your way too. Bonds is a great baseball player and I respect what he is doing.

It seems as though some of the most legendary stories about baseball have something to do with Leroy "Satchel" Paige.

Mobile was a good baseball town and it all started with Old Satch. He inspired us because we used to go down there and watch him play. When the major league teams would barnstorm during the off-season, the amateur teams in Mobile would ask my brother Franklin and me to play. I remember how nice it was to walk into those clubhouses to see those major league guys and how they carried themselves. It was great. I got a chance to face Joe Black, a terrific right-handed pitcher for the Brooklyn Dodgers, when I was 15 or 16 years old. I didn't strike out against him, I remember that much. I hit it somewhere and that gave me confidence.

My second year in baseball, I had the opportunity to barnstorm with Paige. We got about five or six guys from

Mobile and we took a bus to go to Florida, where we picked up some more guys to join our team. We went to St. Petersburg, and Ed Charles, who later was a member of the 1969 New York Mets, was one of the players on the other team. We would start playing those games and then, in about the fifth or sixth inning, Satch would roll up in his white Cadillac. He would stroll down to the bench and say to one of the catchers, "Hey, let's go down to the bullpen and see if I can throw a strike."

Satch would then take out a piece of chewing gum and ball it up. Then he would tell the catcher, "Sit behind that piece of gum wrapper on the ground and let's see how many I can throw over that."

Then Paige, who was a string bean of a man—about 6'4" and 180 pounds soaking wet—with enormous hands, would proceed to throw strikes, one after another. He had such good control. Then he would come in the game and pitch the last two innings. He did that in a lot of cities. We didn't have radar guns back then to measure the speed of pitches, but I would estimate that Satch could throw the ball about 95 miles an hour with pinpoint control.

Aaron's personality has not changed one bit throughout the many years. He was always soft-spoken and deliberate with everything he did.

Satchel used to call me "Young Blood." I was about 19 years old then. Satch, who was also a pretty good hitter, would say to me, "Let me show you how to hit, Young Blood."

In addition to playing baseball, Satch also loved to fish. Sometimes we would go to the trunk of his car to get extra bats and balls. But as we opened up the trunk, often he would have a fish in there that he had forgotten to take out. The putrid smell would just knock you out.

I had the pleasure of presenting Satchel for the Mobile Hall of Fame. His sister accepted the award on his behalf. She told me, "Satch was a good ballplayer, but I think my other brother was a better ballplayer. He liked baseball, too, but he liked girls better."

We didn't have radar guns back then to measure the speed of pitches, but I would estimate that Satch could throw the ball about 95 miles an hour with pinpoint control.

By the time blacks were allowed to play in the major leagues, Satch was 42 years old. He pitched for the Cleveland Indians in 1948 and had a 6–1 record as the Indians went on to win the World Series. The Indians had signed him in midseason. He pitched a total of six big-league seasons with the Indians, St. Louis Browns, and Kansas City Athletics, and he was selected to two All-Star teams. His career record was 28–31 with a very impressive earned run average of 3.29. It's too bad the rest of America couldn't have seen him at his very best during his twenties and thirties.

The last time that I saw old Satch was when I was in the big leagues and staying at the Evans Hotel in Chicago. I stopped up in his room and we shared some laughs and great memories. It was good to see him again. He died June 8, 1982, at the age of 76 in Kansas City, Missouri. I am glad he lived to enjoy being inducted into the Hall of Fame in 1971.

Of course, when I think of Satchel Paige, I also think about the legendary Ted "Double Duty" Radcliffe, also a native of Mobile. He succumbed to cancer at the age of 103. I had gotten to know Double Duty very well over the years, and I heard so many of the stories surrounding his amazing career in baseball. He lived in Chicago much of his life and came out to many ballgames at both Wrigley Field and U.S. Cellular Field on the (formerly Comiskey Park) South Side , where the White Sox play.

He was an All-Star catcher and pitcher in the Negro Leagues for half a century, including a stint with the Chicago American Giants in the 1930s and '40s. He played in Negro League Baseball All-Star games in front of 50,000 people at the old Comiskey Park. He also played in an exhibition

When he takes off his uniform for the last time, Bonds will be regarded as one of the greatest players who ever played.

game against the Cubs in 1945 at Wrigley Field when the Cubs would go on to win the National League pennant.

After starring as a pitcher and a catcher, Radcliffe became a manager.

New York American sportswriter Damon Runyon gave him the nickname "Double Duty" because Radcliffe performed as a catcher and as a pitcher in successive games of a 1932 Negro League World Series doubleheader between the Pittsburgh Crawfords and the Monroe Monarchs at Yankee Stadium.

Radcliffe caught for Paige for a shutout in the first game, then pitched a shutout in the second game. Runyon wrote that Radcliffe "was worth the price of two admissions." Radcliffe considered his year with the 1932 Pittsburgh

Crawfords to be one of the highlights of his career. The Crawfords beat the Monarchs 5–1 in the nine-game series.

Radcliffe pitched three and caught three of the six East-West All-Star games in which he played. He also pitched in two and caught in six other All-Star games. He hit .376 in nine exhibition games against major leaguers, years before blacks were allowed to play in the major leagues.

Once in her career, Stone got a hit off of Paige and called it the happiest moment in her life.

Born July 7, 1902, in Mobile, Radcliffe began his professional career with the Detroit Stars in 1928. He went on to play for the St. Louis Stars (1930), Homestead Grays (1931), Pittsburgh Crawfords (1932), Columbus Blue Birds (1933), New York Black Yankees, Brooklyn Eagles, Cincinnati Tigers, Memphis Red Sox, Birmingham Black Barons, Chicago American Giants, Louisville Buckeyes, and Kansas City Monarchs. Radcliffe managed the Cleveland Tigers in 1937, Memphis Red Sox in 1938, and the Chicago American Giants in 1943.

His biographer, Kyle P. McNary, estimated that Radcliffe had a .303 batting average, 4,000 hits, and 400 homers in 36 years in the game.

At 5' 9" and weighing 210 pounds, Radcliffe was remembered as having a strong throwing arm and good reflexes. He was known to throw many pitches now known to be illegal, including the emery ball, the cut ball, and the spitter.

Radcliffe was one of 10 children. One of his brothers, Alex, also achieved renown as a ballplayer, playing third base. His oldest brother, Earnest, lived to be 105.

He told me the Radcliffe boys used to play baseball using a taped ball of rags with their friends, including Paige and Bobby Robinson.

Ted told me that he and Alex hitchhiked north to Chicago in 1919 to join an older brother. The rest of the family soon followed to live on the South Side of Chicago. A year later, Ted signed with the semi-pro Illinois Giants for $50 for every 15 games and 50 cents a day meal money. This worked out to about $100 a month. He traveled with the Giants for a few seasons before joining Gilkerson's Union Giants, another semi-pro team with whom he played until he joined the Detroit Stars in 1928 and entered the Negro National League.

Radcliffe was the regular catcher for the Detroit Stars for the first half of the season. When the pitching staff became weary toward the end of the season, he began pitching and helped lead the team to a championship. His career-best batting average was .316 for the 1929 Detroit Stars.

The 1931 Homestead Grays, according to Radcliffe, were the greatest team of all time. That team included Josh Gibson, Oscar Charleston, Jud Wilson, and "Smokey Joe" Williams. Gibson and Charleston joined him on the 1932 Pittsburgh Crawfords.

My brother was in the Georgia State League with Willie "Stretch" McCovey. When they first started playing against each other, Franklin didn't realize that McCovey was from the Mobile region. Then they got to talking one day and Franklin found out that McCovey is from nearby Maysville, and of course we are from Whistler. They had some good times when they played against each other. And when McCovey came back to the Mobile area, we would all play basketball together. He's 6'4" with very long arms, so you can imagine how tough he was to guard in basketball. We did a lot of things together. Before he was married, Willie would pick up his girlfriend at Alabama State and we would ride up there with him many times. And McCovey would come to my house in Whistler often as we relaxed and just enjoyed life. Times just seemed so much simpler then.

We had about 15 guys from the area who would get together regularly just before the start of spring training.

A man named Jessie Thomas from Mobile scouted and signed McCovey for the Giants.

McCovey was part of a powerful Giants lineup, along with Mays. Many observers consider McCovey to have been one of the 10 best left-handed hitters of all time. He was National League Rookie of the Year 1959 with a .354 batting average and 13 homers in just 52 games. And McCovey also won the National League MVP award in 1969 after hitting 45 home runs, driving in 126, and batting .320. McCovey wound down his marvelous 22-year career with 521 homers and a .270 batting average.

I will remember McCovey as an easygoing, down-home kid who made it big, yet never let the success go to his head. I am so glad that the Giants organization has recognized what he means to that franchise. They even named the area of water beyond the right-field fence of their new ballpark "McCovey Cove." That is where he would have deposited many of his 521 career homers.

Ozzie Smith was born in Mobile on December 26, 1954. I was already in high school at that time. But he would become known as the greatest defensive player of all time. He earned the nickname "The Wizard of Oz" en route to the Hall of Fame. He won 13 consecutive Gold Gloves and made 15 All-Star Game appearances.

Willie Mays was born outside of Birmingham, in Westfield, Alabama, but we claim "The Say Hey Kid" as one of our own. Mays was a two-time MVP who made an incredible 24 All-Star Game appearances in his Hall of Fame career. He was a 12-time Gold Glove winner. Mays led the NL in home runs four times, triples three times, and stolen bases four times.

Another superb athlete from my state is Bo Jackson, who was born in Bessemer, Alabama. He had been a star at Auburn University in football, baseball, and track and field.

On the professional level, he excelled in both football and baseball. He was a running back for the Raiders and a slugging outfielder with the Chicago White Sox. Unfortunately, he injured his hip playing football and never regained his phenomenal skills.

Cleon Jones was from nearby Plateau, Alabama. He made his major league debut in 1963 with the Mets. He played for New York for 12 years, then finished up with the White Sox before hanging up his spikes in 1976. He was the opposite of me in that he threw left-handed and batted right-handed.

He had decent power, but not great. And his career batting average was a very respectable .281. His best year was 1969, when he batted .340 and drove in 75 runs. That was the year the Mets overtook us late in the season and went on to win the World Series. I never did hear the end of that from Cleon. He was inducted into the New York Mets Hall of Fame in 1991, and I am sure he is quite proud of that. It had to be a pleasure for him to play so many years with the Mets alongside his childhood friend Tommie Agee.

I remember when Cleon had a run-in with his manager, Gil Hodges, in '69. Hodges felt Cleon was not hustling on a play in the outfield, so he walked out of the dugout to the outfield to take Cleon out of the game.

But if it wasn't for Cleon's terrific play in '69, where would the Mets have finished? He made his lone All-Star Game appearance in 1969. Even in the World Series that year he was a big factor. In the fifth game of the World Series Cleon claimed he was hit by a pitch. The home-plate umpire denied him first base. But this time Hodges came out of the dugout to actually support Jones. Hodges pointed out that the baseball had a scuff mark on it from hitting Jones's shoe. So he was awarded first base and the Mets went on to win the World Series that day.

Amos Otis was a terrific all-around player who enjoyed a productive 17-year career in the big leagues. He made the American League All-Star team five times and won three Gold Gloves in center field. He was also a prolific base stealer. We called him by the nickname "A.O." He was originally drafted by the Red Sox, who left him unprotected the next year—when the Mets signed him. He was on their 1969 World Series roster, but played most of his career with the Kansas City Royals. He stole 341 bases in his career, including 52 in 1971. And he had a career batting average of .277.

In 1971 he stole five bases in one game, an incredible feat. It was the first time any player had accomplished that in 44 years. Amos was also an outstanding fielder, perfecting the one-handed catch in the outfield.

Tommie Agee had a nice 12-year career in the big leagues, making the All-Star team twice as a member of the Chicago White Sox. He stole 44 bases, hit 22 homers, and batted .273 in 1966 for the White Sox to win American League Rookie of the Year honors. And he had some outstanding years with the Mets, including 1969, when he batted .271 with 26 homers.

Milt Bolling was a contemporary of mine in Mobile, although the white amateur teams did not play the black teams back then. Milt also played his major league career in the American League from 1952–58. He was a right-handed-hitting infielder, known more for his defensive ability than his offense. He had a .240 career batting average.

All of us came from humble, hard-working families who made tremendous sacrifices to make sure we had the opportunity to succeed in baseball and in life.

Milt's younger brother, Frank Bolling, played 12 years in the big leagues. He was a second baseman for the Tigers before being traded to the Milwaukee Braves in 1960. I played against him many times when the Cubs faced Milwaukee, and then the Atlanta Braves. He was a solid and respected player.

Frank and Milt played together briefly in the late 1950s with Detroit, a rare double-play team of brothers.

Milt signed a pro contract right out of high school at the age of 17. His mother wanted him to go college, so he later attended Spring Hill College during the off-seasons right there in Mobile. He graduated from that Jesuit school in 1954. At the conclusion of his playing career,

Milt worked as a scout and a front-office executive for the Red Sox.

All in all, I think we have done the city of Mobile proud. All of us came from humble, hard-working families who made tremendous sacrifices to make sure we had the opportunity to succeed in baseball and in life. I cannot stress enough how grateful I am to my parents for the encouragement they gave me over the years to do the best I could with the God-given talent I was blessed to possess. And the same can be said for my wife, Shirley, and our children: Valarie, Nina, Julia, and Sandra. They have all displayed tremendous patience and understanding while I went out to pursue my dream profession.

I feel that my values are in the right place and my appreciation for what I was able to accomplish on the baseball diamond could not be greater.

Baseball was my life growing up, and it still is. I think about it when I am driving home from work and I think about it when I am home. My wife and I talk about it. It has just been a part of my life.

So many people think only of the glitz and glamour associated with professional sports, particularly in today's era. But times were dramatically different in the 1950s and '60s when the money was not extravagant and we were driven almost exclusively by the love of the game.

But if I had it to do all over again, I would not change a thing. I feel that my values are in the right place and my appreciation for what I was able to accomplish on the baseball diamond could not be greater.

When I was in my prime as a ballplayer, I surely didn't think I would be in baseball when I was 69 years old. But baseball grabbed me. As a matter of fact, when I first came into the big leagues, I said I was going to play 10 years and then I was going to retire. But I have enjoyed the game so much. I have spent close to 50 years in the game of baseball. And I am still enjoying it.

CHAPTER 4

My Chicago Cubs Teammates from A to Z

Oh, the stories I could tell!

During my 16 years as a player with the Cubs organization, I had the opportunity to meet and really get to know some particularly fascinating individuals. Most of you Cubs fans already know by heart the statistics of your favorite players. But what about their personalities off the field, their peculiar habits in the clubhouse and on the many planes and buses we had to ride? What about their social lives, their families and friends?

I have pretty much seen all types of individuals during my many years in baseball, from the eccentric to the humorous to the painfully shy and reserved. In this chapter, I thought I would try to give you a glimpse of what it was like to live with many of your favorite Cubs ballplayers from my era. Many of them remain lifelong friends of mine.

They all shared a zest for the game of baseball and an appreciation for the devotion of loyal Cubs fans. Over my many years of playing baseball on Chicago's North Side, I often said to myself, "I wish I had a camera to record what I am witnessing, because nobody else would believe what I am seeing." Or, "One day I should write a book about the many things I have seen and experienced during my life in baseball."

Well, I cannot go back in time and take pictures of what I saw, but I can still write a book and try to paint a mental picture with some of the many recollections that I have of Chicago Cubs baseball in the 1960s and '70s.

Do you have change for 3 cents?

Ernie Banks was a terrific Hall of Fame ballplayer and a super human being. But when it came to being a quiet, easygoing room-mate...well, I took a pass on that idea after just a few weeks of my rookie year.

> I have pretty much seen all types of individuals during my many years in baseball, from the eccentric to the humorous to the painfully shy and reserved.

When I first met Ernie in Mesa, Arizona, during spring training in 1958, I found him to be one of the most talented guys that you would ever want to meet. We had a lot of fun together...Ernie, Tony Taylor, and me.

Ernie always has made up those strange rhymes and slogans that we all have heard him recite over the years. A lot of them didn't make much sense. He would say things such as, "The Cubs will shine in '69." Then he would say other things to us players in the clubhouse or in the dugout that nobody could figure out, such as, "Do you have change for three cents?" or "The weather will be cold, the weather will be hot. There will be weather, whether or not."

I got a chance to room with Ernie when I first joined the club. That lasted about three weeks, until after I got all the information I needed from him about the pitchers in the major leagues.

I remember waking up in our team hotel in Houston at about 5:30 or 6:00 AM. That's when I discovered that Ernie was an early riser. I looked over and saw his bed was empty. He was up early that morning talking with his father, who was in the room too. Ernie grew up in Dallas, so it made sense that his family would come to Houston to see him play. But did they have to visit at 5:30 in the morning?

Ernie always kept up with current events and he could talk intelligently about anything that was going on. I never did see him read a book but he always read the paper. Ernie was fun to play baseball with, but he was not especially fun to room with. He would stay up all night talking baseball. Also, Ernie was really into golf and I wasn't into golf at the time. I think Fergie Jenkins later got Ernie as a roommate.

Ernie Banks was a terrific Hall of Fame ballplayer and a super human being.

Ernie was raised in the South and endured at least as much racism as I did during the late 1940s and early '50s. He had played for the Kansas City Monarchs of the Negro Leagues before the Cubs signed him to a contract.

The racism bothered him but I never heard him say anything about it publicly. There would be times when we would have a conversation and he would talk about racist things that happened to him. For instance, he thought that it was a racial thing because Jack Sanford of the Giants used to hit him almost every time he pitched. That's because Ernie used to hit a lot of home runs off Jack Sanford too.

In Chicago, Ernie and I used to ride back and forth from the ballpark to our homes on the South Side, and he would talk about discriminatory things that had happened to him in the past, but never publicly.

Ernie was married during the first couple of years in the big leagues. He had gotten married at a young age to a girl down in Dallas while he was playing with the Kansas City Monarchs. He was going through a big problem with her when he first came up to the Cubs in 1953. Through the help of the Cubs and Mr. Wrigley, they quietly resolved the divorce situation so that Ernie would not worry too much. I think she was paid off by the Cubs and Ernie was free of everything.

After he had separated from her, it was a long time before Ernie got married again, this time to Elois.

When Ernie and Elois separated, it was in the newspapers that she was selling a lot of his trophies and memorabilia. According to an article in *JET* magazine, 85 trophies and mementos of Banks were sold to the highest bidders in Chicago. He had lost those items in the divorce settlement with Elois.

He lost his 500th home-run ball, a sterling silver bat, and a 4-foot-high trophy commemorating his 500th home run. Those three items alone sold for a total of $40,500. He also lost possession of his Hall of Fame plaque for $8,500 and Hall of Fame pin for $4,750. When the bidding came to an end, 85 of Ernie's possessions had been auctioned off for a total of $82,000.

Ernie was the National League Most Valuable Player in 1958 and 1959 while playing shortstop, even though our teams were not very good. He played shortstop from 1953 to 1961. From 1962 to 1971 he was a first baseman, a position at which he showed excellent range and a strong arm. A first-ballot Hall of Famer, Banks played his entire career with the Cubs (1953–1971). He was a 15-time All-Star and won a Gold Glove at shortstop in 1960.

If we had played in the era of free agency, Ernie and I certainly could have made many millions of dollars. But I would not trade the experiences we enjoyed.

Nervous Energy

We used to call Glenn Beckert, our steady-hitting second baseman, "Bruno." The nickname just somehow seemed to fit him. He was always bumping into stuff. And it seemed like he was always doing things off the field that would make you walk away scratching your head and wondering how he got himself into that predicament. Yet he always managed to get himself out of scrapes and land on his feet and end up okay. He came out smelling like a rose.

If we had played in the era of free agency, Ernie and I certainly could have made many millions of dollars.

He also was the nervous type off the field. He couldn't keep still. If we were taking a short flight from Chicago to St. Louis, for instance, Beckert couldn't sit down for five minutes. He always had to get up and walk around. He was always that way, and he still is. The other guys on the Cubs would take bets on how long it would take Beckert before he would get up and start walking around somewhere.

Several decades later, Beckert remains the same. A few of us former Cubs have tried to sit down and have an extended conversation with Beckert at the annual Cubs Conventions that we have now. He will sit down for about five minutes and then hop up and start walking around. He just can't keep still.

Most of the guys on the team back then were smokers. And Beckert was a guy who would bum matches and cigarettes off you if he could to grab a smoke. Then he would run off with the matches and cigarettes.

Not only was he quick on his feet, but Beckert was a quick-witted guy, and he is still quick-witted.

> **Not only was he quick on his feet, but Beckert was a quick-witted guy, and he is still quick-witted.**

And as a ballplayer, Beckert was always very dependable. He might not have been the smoothest, most graceful-looking fielder at second base, but he always got the job done. He had decent, but not exceptional, range. He was a four-time All-Star during his stint with the Cubs from 1965–73.

Beckert was the kind of player you had to have in the lineup because of his bat and willingness to do whatever it took to win. I remember that he was an especially key player for us in 1969, when he hit .291. And I recall that he got hurt midway through the season before returning and continuing to contribute. He was a .283 career hitter, and he only struck out about 25 times a year. In 1971 he had a career year and hit .342.

Beckert and Ron Santo roomed together on the road for many years. After we lost our division to the Mets in heartbreaking fashion in 1969, Beckert and Ronnie decided to get away from it all by traveling to Las Vegas for fun and relaxation. The last thing they wanted to do was watch the hated Mets play in the World Series that year against the

Baltimore Orioles. Well, as it turned out, while Beckert and Santo got ready to play at the blackjack table, the casino operators opened up a 100-foot screen right in front of them, showing the Mets and Orioles playing in the World Series. To say the least, neither Ronnie nor Beckert was very happy to see that.

Beckert and Randy Hundley have both done a good job of staying in touch with all of their former Cubs teammates throughout the years. I get a call from Beckert almost every other week. The last call I got from him, he was up in Anchorage, Alaska, fishing. He calls to see how I am doing and to talk about the current Cubs ballclub.

Beckert was the kind of player you had to have in the lineup because of his bat and willingness to do whatever it took to win.

When he was younger, Glenn used to look a lot like Paul Newman, who was a very popular actor of those days. So the young girls loved him and Beckert played that role to the hilt.

As Cubs players, we all used to protect each other on the field. Mike Shannon used to play a real tough, hard-nosed brand of baseball for the St. Louis Cardinals back in our day. One game, Shannon went in real hard at second base to break up a double play. He hit Beckert and knocked him up in the air about eight feet. He hit him pretty good. So, in order for Beckert to stay in the lineup that day, he had to take some painkilling medication from the trainer. Later that night, Santo told the rest of us that during that game, Beckert was actually singing while he was positioned on the infield and saying, "Hit the ball to me, hit the ball to me!"

Apparently the pills he had been given during the game made Beckert react that way. He was a little loopy. That was kind of funny.

A Friend to the End

Jim Brewer was a great friend of mine. He was from Broken Arrow, Oklahoma, and he was a left-handed pitcher. When I first went off to play pro ball in 1956, I remember meeting Jim's father, whose right arm was cut off at the elbow. His father would come to watch Jim play all of the time.

> **Jim Brewer always looked out for me.**

Out of the 25 guys on that minor league ballclub, five guys got a chance to come to the major leagues. That was a rarity. Lou Johnson, Sammy Drake, Chick Greenwood, Russ Gregg, and I got a chance.

Jim Brewer always looked out for me. I was not allowed to eat in a lot of the whites-only restaurants back then, but Jim would bring food out to me in the buses we rode. I believe Jim was part Native American. In spring training the players used to play cards in the barracks, where they had army cots. I remember Jim and another guy playing cards one night. I was almost asleep, but Jim got mad at somebody who was playing. The next thing I knew, Jim had this guy pinned up against the wall. Jim did not take much BS.

In 1960 Brewer had his jaw broken by Billy Martin, who was with the Cincinnati Reds then. I think Jim had thrown the ball close to Martin, probably in retaliation for a Cubs player being hit or brushed back. Jim always protected the guys who drove in runs for him.

On the second strike to Martin, his bat slipped out of his hands and landed near the pitching mound. Brewer reached down to give Martin the bat. That's when Martin sucker punched Brewer and broke his jaw. Someone held Brewer back after the punch, but I think if he had gotten to Martin, he would have killed him. That's the kind of individual he was. I had seen Brewer get into scrapes during Class D ball in the minors with other teams.

After Martin punched him, Brewer was out of action for a long time.

Brewer and former Dodgers player Bill Russell were both from Broken Arrow. Recently, Russell had a shirt that Brewer used to wear and he sent it to Brewer's widow. Brewer was killed in an automobile accident when he was just 50.

The Trade That Made History

The mere mention of Lou Brock's name causes pain and regret on the part of longtime Cubs fans worldwide.

When baseball fans talk about the worst trades of all time, the controversial 1964 deal sending a young Brock to the St. Louis Cardinals in exchange for veteran right-handed pitcher Ernie Broglio comes up.

The result was that Brock became a Hall of Fame outfielder for the Cardinals, collecting more than 3,000 hits and stealing 938 bases. Broglio went 7–19 in three disappointing years with the Cubs.

But at the time, in my opinion, it was a good trade. And I will still say that because we had other guys swinging the bat well and scoring a lot of runs. We needed pitching and Ernie Broglio had won 18 games for the Cardinals in 1963 and 20 games for them in 1960. But we didn't know that something was wrong with his arm when he came over to Chicago. And Lou hadn't proven himself as being a Major League Baseball player at that point with the Cubs. We just knew he had speed.

On the day in 1964 that the Cubs traded Brock to the Cardinals, I was participating in a golf tournament with Ron Santo and Cubs executive Bob Kennedy. When we got to one of the holes, someone came out there to meet us in a golf cart and said that Bob was wanted in the clubhouse for an important phone call from Wrigley Field. It was John Holland calling.

Kennedy returned to the golf course and Santo and I were trying to get him to tell us what happened with the mysterious phone call, but he wouldn't say anything at the time. Later on that evening, following our golf outing, we found out that Lou had been traded for Broglio. Brock had been signing autographs at a store in Chicago during that off day and could not be reached immediately to be notified of the trade. I guess that's why Kennedy didn't want Santo and me to hear about the transaction first.

Lou was a good kid, and he and I used to room together in Arizona during spring training.

He had this little 8mm projector and we looked at a lot of films in the evening after we had our workouts at the ballpark.

As a veteran at the time, I had a car in Arizona and he didn't, so I would let him use mine quite a bit at night. As a young ballplayer, he had a lot of speed to steal bases. You could see the talent.

But there was a fundamental difference in his approach to the game with the Cardinals, compared to his short stint in the Cubs organization.

When Lou would come to the plate, most of the Cubs coaching staff would tell him—because he had such great speed and he was a left-handed hitter—"Try to hit the ball to the shortstop and run like hell. Either do that, or bunt." That's what he heard all of the time from our coaches.

Lou would tell me that he couldn't play that way. When he went to St. Louis, their manager, Johnny Keane, told Lou to just play baseball and have fun. Lou told me later that piece of advice was the thing that really turned his career as a baseball player around.

We certainly didn't know [Brock] was that kind of ballplayer before we traded him.

When he went to the plate with St. Louis, if he saw the third baseman playing back, Lou would bunt. And here is a guy who wound up hitting almost 150 home runs and who got more than 3,000 hits on the way to the Hall of Fame. We certainly didn't know he was that kind of ballplayer before we traded him.

Ray of Hope

Ray Burris was drafted by the Detroit Tigers out of high school, but he elected to go to college at Southwestern Oklahoma State University. The Cubs drafted him in 1972, and he played with us through 1979.

He would win 15 games in 1975 and again in 1976. Those would be the two winningest seasons of his 15-year career. I really got to know Ray better when we were both in Oakland in 1984. I was a coach then. I stayed with him in an apartment in Oakland that the A's Mitchell Paige owned. He didn't even charge us any rent.

Ray was always doing things in the business world and had a lot of good things going on in his life. He currently has a sports academy in Fort Worth, Texas.

He was a good athlete, and managers often used Ray as a pinch-runner on days that he was not scheduled to pitch. I remember that he was planning to retire after the 1986 season and serve as the Milwaukee Brewers' pitching coach. The Brewers talked him into pitching in 10 games in 1987.

Jose, Can You See?

I think I was the only one who could get away with calling Jose Cardenal "hot dog." That was a name I gave him when he first came into the league with the San Francisco Giants. It seemed like he added a little flair from his native Cuba to whatever he was doing, whether he was catching a routine fly ball or stealing a base or laying down a bunt.

As a member of the Cubs, one of the things I always did was have a party at my house in suburban Glen Ellyn, Illinois, for any of the new black ballplayers who joined the team, just to make them feel welcome. Shirley loved to cook and she would fix a big meal. So Cardenal and his first wife, Pat, would come out to the house.

We would always have a different theme for the parties. One time it might be a Hawaiian theme, and everybody would wear the appropriate clothing. Jose and his wife always seemed to enjoy those parties. Pat was the type of person who wouldn't take any mess off of anybody.

One time I saw Pat and her daughter walk into the ball-park—because there weren't a whole lot of people coming to most games at Wrigley Field in the early '60s. All of a sudden I saw her pointing her finger at an usher and arguing. At that point, as I am coming off the field at the end of an inning, I got Shirley's attention in the stands so that she could go down and straighten out the situation.

Jose wasn't a big guy, about 5'10" and 165 pounds. But he could hit the ball out of the ballpark like a lot of the big guys. He had one of the best arms in the major leagues as a center fielder. But he was also rather eccentric. Just for fun, he would hide baseballs out in the vines that cover the outfield walls of Wrigley Field before some of the games.

Cardenal missed a Cubs exhibition game in 1974 when he said his eyelid was stuck shut.

Often, it would appear that he was loafing out in the field, but he was a good ballplayer. He got the job done. And he had so much hair that it seemed as though his cap didn't stay on his head that much. Cardenal also played for the Mets, Angels, Cardinals, Brewers, Indians, Phillies, Giants, and Royals during his 18 years in the big leagues.

He was the Cubs' right fielder in 1973 when he led the team in hitting (.303), doubles (33), and steals (19). Chicago baseball writers named Cardenal the "Chicago Player of the Year" that season.

Cardenal is a cousin of former big-league shortstop Bert Campaneris, who was a teammate of mine with the Oakland A's in 1975.

The Brewers traded Cardenal to the Cubs in 1971 for pitcher Jim Colborn and two other players.

Cardenal spent six seasons in Chicago and was considered one of our most popular players. In 1972, I remember Cardenal had a triple, double, and two singles against the Braves.

In a 14-inning win over the Giants in 1976, Cardenal went 6-for-7 at the plate, including a double and a home run, driving in four runs.

In 2001 Cardenal was accused by Pete Rose of using a corked bat. Rose was his teammate on the 1979 Phillies.

"I did have a corked bat one time," Rose told ESPN. "You know who corked them? Jose Cardenal. I never used it in a game. But we'd come in the clubhouse in Philly, and Jose Cardenal would be corking bats. You'd hear the drill going—zizzzzzzzzzzzz. But I never used none of them bats in a game."

What's in Your Wallet?

Rico Carty used to call himself "The Beeg Boy." He could really hit, banging out more than 200 homers while hitting around .300 for his 15-year career.

His stay with the Cubs in 1973 was quite brief, but one unique thing about Rico Carty really sticks out in my mind.

Rico never trusted anybody in the clubhouse when it came to the safety of his personal valuables. In the Cubs' locker room all of the other guys would place their wallets, watches, and jewelry in a security box and it was locked up safely in the clubhouse. If you look at any old films of Rico Carty playing baseball, you will see a big wad in the back pocket of his uniform pants. That was his wallet. Apparently, he wanted his wallet and cash with him at all times, even on the base paths, in the outfield, and in the batter's box.

By the time he joined the Cubs in 1973, Carty already had suffered a bout of tuberculosis that caused him to miss the entire 1968 season. He had starred initially with the Braves. He also played for Cleveland, Texas, Oakland, and finally Toronto.

He hit .330 with 22 homers as a rookie in 1964 finishing second to Roberto Clemente in batting and second to Dick Allen for Rookie of the Year. He was known as a fancy dresser, owning dozens of suits and flashy outfits. He loved baseball and played year-round in the winter leagues. But he injured his knee badly during a collision in the outfield and had to sit out the 1971 season. During that year of rehabbing Rico was roughed up by an off-duty policeman in Atlanta. His eye was damaged in that fracas and the policeman involved was suspended.

Carty was born in San Pedro de Macoris, Dominican Republic, the same small hometown of Sammy Sosa and Alfonso Soriano. Carty was even named an honorary general in the Dominican army.

If it hadn't been for the injuries and serious illness that he had to endure, Rico's career numbers might have been good enough to get him into the Hall of Fame.

Fiery Manager

He played in only 15 games as a utility infielder for the Cubs in 1968 and batted .176, but Lee Elia was the kind of guy you could never forget. He also would have been a teammate of mine on the 1969 Cubs team, but he was traded to the Yankees in April of that year.

Elia had an inauspicious big-league playing career with the White Sox in 1966 and then the Cubs. But most baseball fans will always remember him for being the fiery manager of the Cubs.

In April of 1983, Elia lost his cool and delivered a profanity-filled tirade to the press following a loss to the Pirates at Wrigley Field. The team was off to a slow start and a small crowd booed the team as they left the field. I think some of the players had beer and other debris thrown at them as they were walking down the left-field foul line toward the clubhouse.

At that point, Elia just lost it. "What the [bleep] am I supposed to do, go out there and let my [bleep]ing players get destroyed every day and be quiet about it?" Elia said. "For the [bleep]ing nickel-dime people who turn up? The [bleep]ers don't even work. That's why they're out at the [bleep]ing game. They oughta go out and get a [bleep]ing job and find out what it's like to go out and earn a [bleep]ing living. Eighty-five percent of the [bleep]ing world is working. The other 15 percent come out here."

A tape-recorded version of the tirade is often played on the radio, with all of the profanity edited out, of course.

Elia had a 73–89 record managing the Cubs in 1982 as the team finished in fifth place. He was fired as manager of the Cubs in August of 1983 and replaced on an interim basis by Charlie Fox. The Cubs were 54–69 when Elia was fired. The team had been just three-and-one-half games out of first place at the All-Star break.

In 1984 Jim Frey took over as Cubs manager and led them to a surprise first-place finish in the NL East. Elia received another opportunity to manage in the middle of the 1987 season with the Phillies. He had a 51–50 record with them that season, but slipped to 60–92 in 1988 when Philadelphia wound up in sixth place. His career managerial record was 238–300 for a .442 winning percentage.

Stranger Than Fiction

You get some memorable characters in the game of baseball, and Bill Faul certainly was one of them.

Bill wore No. 13 when he pitched for the Cubs, and he used to dabble in hypnotism. There was even a story going around that he once ate a live frog.

When we traveled to road games, many times Faul would try to hypnotize one of the stewardesses. I am not sure if he was ever able to do it. But one time our team was staying in the Waldorf Astoria Hotel in New York. Faul was on the 19th floor and he told his roommate, Ken Rudolph, that he was going to hypnotize him, turn him into a dog, and make him jump out of the window.

Faul said, "If I'm going to pitch, they are going to have to turn that damn video screen off."

Ken Rudolph was worried to death and he couldn't sleep that night. After that experience, Rudolph stopped rooming with Faul, leaving Faul to stay in hotel rooms by himself.

Another example of Faul's eccentric personality was revealed during a game in the Houston Astrodome. When the Astros were batting and trying to get a rally started, the center-field scoreboard video screen would display these two huge hands clapping as the audio was turned up full blast.

Faul didn't like that, so he backed off the mound and had his back to the plate for a good five minutes, refusing to pitch. Leo Durocher ran out to the mound and said, "Why don't you pitch?"

Faul said, "If I'm going to pitch, they are going to have to turn that damn video screen off."

Despite his bizarre behavior, Faul did manage to pitch three shutout victories for the Cubs in 1965.

Faul was a strange guy, for sure. On the nights that he would pitch, before the games he would go into the training room by himself and turn all the lights off. He would put himself under some kind of spell. We could hear him in there, humming rhythmically to himself. If he went out and pitched well, Faul would say that it was because he put himself in a proper frame of mind. If one of us accidentally went into the training room and turned the lights on to snap him out of his spell before a game—and Faul pitched poorly—he would put the blame on the teammate who turned the lights on.

As a pitcher, one thing Durocher always tried to remind Faul to do was to be in position to field the ball after he delivered the ball. Sure enough, one time we were playing the Giants and Willie McCovey hit a line drive right back at him and in the butt. Faul was a strange character. And his wife was strange too. She would come to Wrigley Field and people said she always carried a pistol in her purse.

Hair Today, Gone Tomorrow

Oscar Gamble used to wear the big Afro hairstyle that barely fit under his baseball cap. He was from Montgomery, Alabama. Nowadays, he owns a big barbecue place in Alabama. He is the only guy I know in Birmingham who drives a white Rolls-Royce. That just fits him because he has always been flamboyant and fancy.

He starred with the Chicago White Sox and the New York Yankees after he came up with the Cubs as a brash 19-year-old. He was an excellent hitter, even though he didn't get that many opportunities to play for the Cubs. But he did a fine job for us. He was always a real confident guy, and he would make sure to tell you that he could hit.

One of his famous quotes was, "When I am at bat, I am in scoring position."

I think it was his flamboyant ways off the field that might have rubbed Leo Durocher the wrong way. At any rate, he was traded to the Phillies after one season with the Cubs. He started showing some power later in his career and belted 31 home runs for the 1977 Chicago White Sox, who were known as the South Side Hitmen.

I don't remember seeing him play the outfield that much with the Cubs. I just remember that squatty stance that he had at the plate. He got some big hits for us. When he ran around town in Chicago, people loved him here.

He has a son named Sean who is with the Phillies organization.

A Man of Few Words and Few Pitches

As a pitcher, Bill Hands had one of the best sliders in the league. He was right there with Carlton Willey and Joey Jay as the guys who had the great sliders.

He came to the Cubs from San Francisco with Randy Hundley. I don't know why the Giants got rid of him, because he was a good young pitcher. He would be right there with Fergie Jenkins doing a tremendous job as a stopper whenever we hit a losing streak. He had great control.

Hands won 20 games for us and led the pitching staff with a 2.49 ERA in 1969. He even had a one-hitter against the Expos in 1972. He certainly was not known for his hitting. He struck out 14 straight times in 1968 to set a dubious major league record.

Personality-wise, he didn't say that much. He just went out there and threw the ball well. Leo loved him because he threw strikes. Leo didn't like anybody who walked a lot of batters. Bill could put a batter away on the fourth or fifth pitch and Leo loved that.

Most pitchers tend to hang out together, separate from a lot of the position players. But Bill and Jim Hickman were friends and they did a lot of stuff together. They had similar personalities, so I guess they could relate to one another.

In our clubhouse, Hands was known as a great chess champion.

Slow to Anger

We obtained Jim Hickman from the Los Angeles Dodgers in 1968 along with reliever Phil Regan. The Cubs sent Ted Savage and Jim Ellis to the Dodgers in exchange.

Nicknamed "Gentleman Jim," Hickman was kind of a quiet guy. The one time I saw him get mad was when he was playing first base while Joe Pepitone was away from the ballclub for five or six days.

Hickman was doing a good job playing first base at the time and when Pepitone returned to the ballclub, Leo Durocher told the press, "Well, Hickman is still the starting first baseman." But about three or four days later, Hickman was back in the outfield and Pepitone was back at first base. That really made Hickman mad. That was the only time I saw him get angry.

Hickman and utility infielder Paul Popovich had lockers right next to each other in the old clubhouse at Wrigley Field. At the end of the clubhouse were lockers for me, Ernie, and Santo. I remember seeing Hickman usually arriving in the clubhouse around 9:30 or 10:00 in the morning for a 1:20 PM game. He would sit there and cross his legs and pick at his toes. Then, about 45 minutes later, he would have on a full uniform. The point is, he wasn't in a hurry to get it done. He would take his time before getting his uniform on.

At 6'4" and about 210 pounds, Hickman was a strong guy with powerful arms. When we would all go golfing, Hickman could hit the ball a long way. He was one of the guys playing the outfield for the Cubs those years that I wanted to out-slug. I didn't want him to hit more home runs than I did during his six years with the Cubs. In 1970 he hit 32 homers. That was the year I hit 42 home runs. In 1971, Hickman hit 19 homers and I hit 28. The balls he hit out of the ballpark were line drives, and I guess he was great motivation for me to do the best I could in the power category.

He was a very good player and made the National League All-Star team in 1970. I remember him having the best arm in our outfield. He wasn't a guy who said much. He just went out and played hard. Every once in a while he would say something funny to the guys on the team, but most of the time he was just out there playing his butt off and letting his performance on the field speak for him.

Watch Out for the Flying Ashtray

Kenny Holtzman had a real contentious contract squabble at one point with the Cubs and general manager John Holland. I understand that they got into a big argument and Holland wound up throwing an ashtray at Holtzman as he was walking out of the office.

Holtzman apparently told Holland, "Look, I am not interested in any individual-type awards or any of that kind of stuff. I want to win. I want to see what it is like to play in a World Series. And I just disagree with the philosophy around here."

Holtzman asked to be traded and they dealt him to Oakland for outfielder Rick Monday. Holtzman later said, "It was like I went to baseball heaven. And, obviously, we won all the time out there."

Holtzman pitched for the Cubs (1965–71, 1978–79), Oakland A's (1972–75), Baltimore Orioles (1976), and New York Yankees (1976–78).

With the A's, Holtzman combined with Vida Blue, Jim "Catfish" Hunter, and John "Blue Moon" Odom to form a great pitching staff, helping the A's to three straight World Series titles. Holtzman was 4–1 with a 2.55 ERA in eight World Series starts.

I noticed that Holtzman seemed to change his pitching style a bit in the American League. When he was with the Cubs, he threw the ball in the low 90s and got a lot of batters out that way. He pitched two no-hitters with the Cubs. But when he got in the American League, he began to throw a lot of breaking balls. I joined him in Oakland in 1974 at the end of my career and got a chance to witness his new style firsthand.

He was quite a character. Durocher saw him in spring training in the early '60s when Kenny was pitching at Class AA, and Leo said, "This kid can win in the big leagues right now." And, of course, he did.

When the Cubs first hired Durocher he brought with him Freddie Fitzsimmons as the pitching coach. Then came Joe Becker. Holtzman and the rest of the Cubs pitchers really seemed to learn a lot from them in terms of mound strategy. Holtzman also has credited Fergie Jenkins and Bill Hands for helping him develop into a top-notch championship-game pitcher.

Holtzman ran around with Ron Santo and Randy Hundley when they were off the field. And Phil Regan was a good friend of his too. All of us played cards together and that was a way for all of us to get to know one another. I recall many times going to Cincinnati for ballgames. It always was tough for us to find a good restaurant that was open there, for some reason. We would say to each other that we were going to play cards for two or three hours and then go out to eat. But often we would end up laughing and playing cards for six or seven hours and eating some sandwiches from the hotel room service menu.

Old Buddy, Burt

I was not surprised to see Ken Holtzman throw two no-hitters for the Cubs during my era. But Burt Hooton's no-hitter against the Phillies in just his fourth major league start seemed to catch everyone off guard.

His no-hitter was a 4–0 victory that featured seven strikeouts and seven walks. Nonetheless, it was a no-hitter and for that he should be congratulated. Burt had a wicked knuckle-curveball pitch that really kept hitters off balance. He threw more than 200 innings in nine different seasons, including more than 239 with the Cubs in 1973.

Hooton pitched in the big leagues for 15 years, including some good years with the Dodgers and Texas Rangers. He was selected by the Cubs in the first round of the amateur draft out of the University of Texas at Austin in 1971. We called him "Happy Hooton."

Burt said his sub-.500 pitching record with the Cubs was due in part to the fact we had three different managers and four different pitching coaches while he was in Chicago.

As a member of the Dodgers, Hooton went 18–7 in 1975 after beginning that season 0–2 with the Cubs. In 1978 he was 19–10. In 1981 he was the Most Valuable Player in the National League Championship Series, the same year that he was named to the NL All-Star team.

Second to None

I thought this guy was going to be one of the greatest base-ball players of all time.

Ken Hubbs, a former roommate of Ron Santo, was named the 1962 National League Rookie of the Year. He hit .260 his first season, nothing too exceptional there, but he had nine triples and stood out defensively by earning a Gold Glove after playing a then-record 78 consecutive errorless games.

He was a native of Colton, California, and on February 13, 1964, Hubbs was killed in a plane crash along with his friend Dennis Doyle during a snowstorm in Provo, Utah. Hubbs, who had been missing for two days before his body was discovered, was just 22.

I remember being back home in Alabama when I turned on the news and heard about the plane crash. It was so sad. I believe his friend was supposed to be getting married, and Kenny was flying him to the place where they were planning to marry.

His brother, Keith Hubbs, said Ken's plane went down in Utah Lake, about two miles from the Provo airport. Keith said his log book was in the plane when Ken crashed. Ken had asked Keith, who already had his pilot's license, to fly with him that day, but their father was trying to talk Ken out of wanting to fly.

Ken was very quiet and unassuming, but he made a loud impact on all the people who saw him play. The Little League in his hometown of Colton is named after him. And the Athlete of the Year honor in the area is named the Ken Hubbs Award. Pro Football Hall of Fame safety Ronnie Lott is among the recipients of the award.

Ken was a Mormon. He played hard. In my mind, he was the same type of player as Hall of Famer Ryne Sandberg, but more aggressive.

A few years ago about 25 members of the Hubbs family flew in from Rialto, California, to Chicago to attend a first-ever "Ken Hubbs Day" at Wrigley Field. The group included Ken's mother, three brothers, and numerous nephews and cousins.

They said Ken was a straight-A student in high school, student body president, and a three-sport all-state athlete.

Keith's 32-year-old son, also named Ken Hubbs, threw out the ceremonial first pitch on June 26, 2002. Ken's 84-year-old mother, Dorothy, and his brothers, Gary and Craig, helped sing "Take Me Out to the Ball Game" during the seventh-inning stretch.

Catch as Catch Can

We called Randy Hundley "The Rebel" because of his strong Southern accent. He was from Martinsville, Virginia. He and J.C. Martin, another former Cubs teammate, were both from that area.

Hundley signed his first big-league contract in 1960 right out of high school.

We got him in a trade with the San Francisco Giants along with starting pitcher Bill Hands. Hundley took the place of Dick Bertell as the Cubs catcher when he was acquired during the off-season of 1965. The Cubs sent Lindy McDaniel and Don Landrum to San Francisco in exchange.

Randy was one of those one-handed catchers, which his Giants manager, Herman Franks, didn't want at the time. But Randy's father had taught him how to catch like that, and Randy convinced Franks and the rest of us that he could get the job done by catching one-handed.

Hundley and Jerry Grote of the Mets always seemed to be competing against each other to be regarded as the best catcher in the National League. Because of that, Randy didn't like Grote. Whenever we played against the Mets, Randy would do everything possible to try to get Grote's attention, just to let him know that he was the better catcher.

Randy had a great way of handling our pitchers and they really respected him. When Leo Durocher became our manager in 1966, he used to really put the pressure on Randy.

I think Durocher tried to intimidate Randy because of his reputation of being a tough manager. For instance, Leo would tell Randy to argue for pitches with the home-plate umpire.

"Get on 'em so you can make them mad enough so I can come out and protect you," Leo would say. Then Leo would tell Randy, "If you don't do it, then I will get somebody else back there who will."

That kind of talk really bothered Hundley, but I think Durocher actually was trying to pay Randy a compliment by trying to make him act as the manager on the field, so to speak. After that first year under Durocher, Randy was able to relax a little more and Durocher didn't seem to ride him as much as that first season.

Randy and Santo used to compete on the golf course a lot, even as players. Hundley still lives in the Chicago area after losing his wife, Betty, to cancer about seven years ago. I know that had to be really tough on him.

Randy started his now-famous Fantasy Baseball Camps in Arizona more than 25 years ago and they are still very popular. It is a wonderful opportunity for a lot of us former Cubs players to continue to interact with fans and get together on an annual basis as well.

Hundley was traded by the Cubs to the Minnesota Twins at the end of the 1973 season for catcher George Mitterwald. Then he signed with San Diego in '75 before returning to the Cubs in 1976.

Randy was a decent hitter with fiery competitiveness and defensive skills. His son, Todd, turned out to be a real power hitter, slugging 41 home runs for the Mets one season, which was then a major league record for catchers. When the Cubs signed Todd to a free-agent contract, it seemed that there was too much pressure on him to perform in his hometown and on the same team his father had starred on in the 1960s and '70s.

Todd had agreed to a $23.5 million, four-year deal to sign with the Cubs. But he struggled and was booed by the Wrigley Field fans. The Cubs then traded him to the Dodgers for Eric Karros and Mark Grudzielanek before the 2003 season.

Oh, Canada!

When Fergie Jenkins came over to the Cubs from Philadelphia in 1966, we hit it off really well right from the start. He had a daughter and I had four daughters. We lived not too far from each other in Chicago, and we often rode back and forth from the ballpark together.

We just enjoyed all of those summers in Chicago together. In the off-season, he would go back to Ontario, Canada. From time to time I would drive up there and go fishing. Or he would come back down to Chicago in the off-season.

When Fergie Jenkins came over to the Cubs from Philadelphia in 1966, we hit it off really well right from the start.

A friend of ours had some land out in suburban Barrington. So Fergie and I would go out there hunting. Fergie liked to do the same types of things that I liked to do: fish and hunt.

When he was in high school in Canada, Fergie competed in track, hockey, and basketball. He once got 14 stitches in his head playing hockey, so his mother made him give up that sport.

His parents were also outstanding athletes when they were younger. His mother had been a great bowler, and his father was a semi-pro baseball player during an era when blacks were not allowed to play Major League Baseball.

Even on the road, Fergie, or "Jenks" as we sometimes called him, and I used to go out to dinner a lot during his 10 years with the Cubs.

He was such a great pitcher and a great athlete. During the off-seasons he would play basketball with the Harlem Globetrotters. I remember one particular night when we were in Pittsburgh. We got back to the hotel really late. Early the next morning, around 5:30 or 6:00 AM, we got up to go fishing. We spent the morning having fun fishing before returning to the team hotel. The team bus was leaving the hotel to go to the ballpark so we ran to our respective rooms to take showers before getting on the bus.

As we were going to the ballpark, I turned around and asked Fergie who was pitching that night. He said, "I am." That surprised me, because if I had known that, we wouldn't have gone fishing. We could have put it off. But Fergie said, "I'm fine." He was a strong individual. I think he went out that night and pitched a two- or three-hitter against the Pirates, which was a good-hitting ballclub at that time. That's the way he was. He ended up with 267 complete games and 49 shutouts among his 284 victories. He won 20 or more games for six years in a row. Amazing!

Not only was he unlucky in the sense of never playing for a championship team in the big leagues, but during his brilliant career, Fergie lost 13 games by the score of 1–0 despite pitching complete games.

I was surprised to hear about his brush with the law in 1980, several years after I was gone from the Cubs. Drugs were found in Fergie's luggage during a road trip to Toronto. Even though the case ultimately was dismissed, he said, "It was about two years before my father believed me when I told him I didn't do it." The baseball commissioner, Bowie Kuhn, suspended Fergie for 20 games, fined him $10,000, and ordered him to take part in Major League Baseball's drug education program.

It was so unfortunate to see the personal tragedies that Fergie had to endure off the field following his playing days. Shirley and I went on a cruise with Fergie and his second wife, Maryanne. She and Fergie were doing real well at first. She was Fergie's second wife, after a divorce from Cathy.

Maryanne was involved in the automobile industry and she was ready to get a dealership. They were having a big party for her at this particular dealership in January of 1991. As she was driving back home the car went off the road and she had a major accident. This was at the same time that Fergie was about to be honored as the first Canadian-born inductee to the National Baseball Hall of Fame in July of 1991.

It was so unfortunate to see the personal tragedies that Fergie had to endure off the field following his playing days.

Maryanne was kept in the hospital to have her broken bones treated (apparently she was not wearing a seat belt at the time of the accident) and she developed pneumonia. She lived through Fergie being inducted into the Hall of Fame but she died in the hospital about 100 hours later.

Fergie would meet another woman who wanted him to marry her right away in Oklahoma. He wasn't ready to take that step just yet, and that really bothered her. His common-law wife was not able to accept that decision. So one day this woman took Fergie's three-year-old daughter, Samantha, whom he had with Maryanne, and drove to an oil field. Fergie thought she was taking his little daughter to preschool.

They drove 30 or 40 miles to find an oil field. I guess there was a pipe that was lying on the ground. She ran this pipe to the exhaust pipe of her car and raised all of the windows. She committed suicide with the little girl in the car. Fergie's daughter also died.

In the meantime, Kenny Holtzman had been trying to contact Fergie about another issue. When Kenny called, someone answered the phone and said, "Fergie can't talk at this time." That's when Holtzman called me and said: "Billy, I don't know what's happening, but why don't you try to give Fergie a call, because it seems like something strange has happened to him."

So I got on the phone to call Fergie in Guthrie, Oklahoma. I told the person who answered who I was and I said, "Let me speak to Fergie." They gave him the phone and we talked. And he told me what had happened. Obviously, it really hurt him. He wasn't ready to get married at the time, and he had gone through a lot of emotions dealing with the loss of his previous wife, Maryanne.

This happened in November of that year. We had the Cubs Fantasy Baseball Camp in January. Randy Hundley invited Fergie to be with most of the '69 Cubs in Arizona. We all went out and sat around, had dinner, and chatted. There must have been at least 12 of us. At the time, Fergie really needed that. To be with the guys he had been with for six months out of every year...he left there a little better than when he came. All of the other players knew what he had gone through.

Fergie's mother was blind and never had a chance to watch him play. She used to listen to his games on a transistor radio. She died of cancer in 1970 at the age of 52. Fergie once said, "Baseball is easy. Life is hard." In fact, that was the title of his autobiography. In the book he writes: "I learned early on that life is fleeting. I buried a mother when she was young, fifty-two. I buried a wife when she was very young, only thirty-two. I buried a daughter when she was only three. I buried a close friend of mine who was in her thirties. I buried my dad who was eighty-nine. In my life I've been a part of many funerals. At one point I told a reporter I should be in a rubber room."

Kick Me Out, Please!

A lot of people don't realize that Lou Johnson was a jockey before he started playing baseball. He was from Lexington, Kentucky. We played together in the minors. His nickname was "Sweet Lou."

One time in Fort Worth, Texas, we had a game scheduled on a very hot day. Lou and I were the only two black players on that team, so they took us to an old hotel on the other side of town. Our room didn't have any air conditioning in it and we were miserable. So we decided to load our bags and went to find one of the better hotels in the black section. We got an air-conditioned suite. The receptionist at the desk asked, "Where are we going to send the bill?" Lou said, "Send it to the Houston Buffaloes." That was the team we were playing for at the time.

Another time we had a game scheduled in Louisville, Kentucky. His mother drove over from Lexington to watch Lou play. In about the fourth or fifth inning, the pitcher threw a ball right down the middle of the plate. But Lou started complaining to the umpire because he wanted to get thrown out of that game. So the home-plate umpire threw him out of the game. The next thing I knew, Lou was sitting in the stands with his mother, waving to me on the field and laughing.

Off the field, Lou was one of the best dancers I had ever seen. But he could also hold his own when guys started to scuffle.

We had a catcher by the name of Ray Nobley, and he and another guy were talking in Spanish in the Flamingo Hotel in Houston. Another person staying at the hotel stuck his head out of his door and said, "Why don't you guys talk in

English?" So they all got into a big fight. I heard the commotion from my hotel room and went out to grab Ray and calm him down. The problem was that Ray was a real big guy and I weighed only about 165 or 170 pounds back then. I could only try to grab Ray around his waist while he had the other guy pinned up against a car. Eventually, Lou Johnson came out there to help me and we got everybody settled down. It was one of those nights.

Lou played with the Cubs in 1960, but he had his best years in the majors with the Los Angeles Dodgers. He rejoined the Cubs for part of the 1968 season. When Sandy Koufax threw a perfect game against us in 1965, Lou got the only hit of the game for the Dodgers off the Cubs' Bob Hendley.

Self-Made Man

I have the utmost respect for Don Kessinger because he made himself a big-league ballplayer.

He didn't have all of the natural talent in the world at first. Kessinger signed with the Cubs out of the University of Mississippi for $25,000. He had great hands and could handle himself defensively with the best of them. But he wasn't a very good offensive player at first.

I remember Leo Durocher telling him during one spring training, "If you make yourself a switch-hitter, then we will have a place for you in the major leagues. All you have to do is hit .250 or .260 because Ernie, Billy, and Ronnie will drive in the runs."

Kessinger went out and did that. He spent another year in the minor leagues and worked really hard on hitting from the left side. He didn't try to pull the ball; he just tried to hit the ball up the middle. By becoming a competent switch-hitter, and with his defensive skills, he made himself an All-Star.

He was a career .252 hitter with only 14 home runs. But Kessinger played 54 consecutive errorless games in 1969, which was then a record for big-league shortstops. He started for the National League in four of the six All-Star games he played in.

He was a great shortstop. He used to be able to go in the hole, jump up in the air, and throw a perfect strike to first base.

In 1969, Kessinger hit .273 to help us lead our division most of the season.

Former Cubs general manager E.R. "Salty" Saltwell traded Kessinger to the St. Louis Cardinals in 1975 for reliever Mike Garman and a minor leaguer. In 1977 he was dealt to the Chicago White Sox. And in a significant career change three years later, the White Sox fired manager Larry Doby and named Kessinger as player-manager for the 1979 season.

A lot of people forget that Kessinger was the manager of the White Sox during "Disco Demolition Night," when thousands of disco records were set on fire during a promotion between games of a doubleheader. Chicago disc jockey Steve Dahl orchestrated the event that resulted in total chaos on the field, and the second game of the double-header had to be postponed. Kessinger said that was one of the scariest moments he could ever remember while in a baseball uniform.

For Pete's Sake
When I injured my ankle in 1972, Pete LaCock was called up from the minors for a couple of weeks.

Pete was sort of a free-spirited guy who happened to be the son of popular game show host Peter Marshall. So a lot of people paid particular attention to him for that reason. He was accustomed to seeing Hollywood types such as Frank Sinatra and Sammy Davis Jr. come to his parents' house when he was growing up. But he also was a pretty decent ballplayer.

He had been the American Association MVP in 1974 after hitting over .320 with 23 homers. The Cubs had selected him in the first round of the 1970 draft as a slugging, left-handed-hitting first baseman.

When he was called up from Double A in 1972, all of us greeted him and tried to make him feel like part of the team right away. I think he really appreciated that.

I remember that Pete would come to the ballpark real early in the morning and let his dog run all around Wrigley Field and up in the stands. I think he lived near the ballpark at the time.

The first day LaCock was in a Cubs uniform, Rick Monday batted against San Diego in the fourth inning. All of a sudden the Padres catcher, Pat Corrales, stood up and punched Monday. Then a bench-clearing, wild fight ensued. LaCock was right in the middle of the fight, even though he wasn't playing that day. That must have really made him feel like he was part of the ballclub.

Pete got his first career big-league hit with the Cubs against Dock Ellis of the Pirates. After the ball was thrown back to the mound, Ellis walked the ball over to LaCock at first base to give it to him as a memento. Pete really appreciated that and the two of them became good friends over the years.

Another one of Pete's claims to fame is that he got the last career hit that Hall of Fame pitcher Bob Gibson gave up. It was a pinch-hit grand slam by LaCock as the Cubs beat the St. Louis Cardinals in 1975.

LaCock went on to play in three League Championship Series with the Royals and one World Series in 1980. But he says his Cubs experience is what he cherishes the most.

"I have been in the playoffs, I have been in the World Series. But nothing compares to the time I had playing at Wrigley Field," said LaCock. "It was the time of my life, being able to play at Wrigley Field."

Managing to Observe

People always talk about how players who sit on the bench to observe the game become good managers. I don't remember too much about Tony LaRussa, the ballplayer, with the Cubs. I know that he was here. But he didn't get a chance to play that much because he was an infielder and we had Glenn Beckert at second base, and if Tony had designs on playing shortstop, we had an All-Star in Don Kessinger. All LaRussa did was sit on the bench and maybe get a chance to pinch-hit every now and then.

It seems to me that Tony LaRussa was a good observer because he has done a great job as a manager. He should become a Hall of Famer as a manager. I remember watching LaRussa as the manager of the White Sox in the 1980s. He and Jim Leyland worked together there when Leyland was a coach. They became really good buddies. I knew that eventually both of them would have managing jobs somewhere. LaRussa did some great things while managing in Oakland and then, of course, St. Louis. Leyland has been a tremendous manager with Pittsburgh, Florida, Colorado, and Detroit.

Over my years in the big leagues, managers had different styles in terms of communicating with their players about in-game strategy and such. Bob Scheffing was a Cubs manager when I first got here and he may have talked to the veteran players during games, but I was new to the ballclub and I had a long way to go. So he certainly didn't spend a lot of time talking to me. Bob Kennedy became the manager and he spent a lot of time talking to players about how to play the game and the various strategies we used.

It seems to me that Tony LaRussa was a good observer because he has done a great job as a manager.

But when it comes to the manager I had who did the most to steer the players and teach them the fundamentals of the game, it was Leo Durocher. He was always two steps ahead of everybody. I would sit down on the bench during a game and talk to him, and he would always let you know his thoughts about what was going to happen next and how he planned to react to a particular situation. He was in control of the game, and it seemed he was in control of the umpires.

Leo even used to get on his coaches and criticize them a lot. The only guy he would not ream out was Joey Amalfitano because every time he would say something to him, Joey would get back at him. One time I asked him, "What do you have on him, Joey?"

I think it goes back to when Leo managed the Giants in 1954 and Joey Amalfitano was a bonus baby. If you signed as a bonus baby back then, you had to stay with the major league ballclub for a year. I think that was when Leo took a liking to Amalfitano.

But LaRussa has become one of the most successful managers in the history of the game, often using unconventional methods to win, including batting the pitcher in the eighth instead of the ninth slot. He and his longtime pitching coach Dave Duncan have worked well together in Chicago, Oakland, and St. Louis. Tony seems to be a very loyal guy when it comes to the people he surrounds himself with, and his teams won World Series titles in both the American and National Leagues.

A Hitting Machine

When Bill Madlock and Vic Harris came to the Cubs from Texas in the trade for Fergie Jenkins in October of 1973, Chicago had an excellent third baseman to take over for Ron Santo.

Madlock won a couple of batting titles with the Cubs, and then two more with the Pirates. A lot of people forget how great a hitter he was. Defensively, he was not Santo at third base, but he got the job done. He was known for swinging the bat and he had a nice, short stroke. And he sprayed the ball all over the field. "Mad Dog," as he was known, had 163 career homers while Santo slugged 342 with a .277 career batting average. Each played for 15 years.

Madlock, who grew up in Decatur, Illinois, wound up playing for six different teams. He was the first player to win more than one batting title with two different teams. He won the crown with the Cubs in 1975 and '76 and the Pirates in 1981 and 1983.

After Bill won his second batting title with the Cubs, I remember going to Salt Lake City, Utah, on business. I was playing handball with Herman Franks, the Cubs manager at the time. After we finished playing, Herman turned to me and said, "I've got to get rid of Madlock."

I said, "You're crazy. Those people will run you out of town if you get rid of that guy."

But apparently something happened between Madlock and the Cubs owner, Mr. Wrigley. And I think Herman was told to get rid of him because of a contract dispute. So they ended up trading Madlock to San Francisco in signing a deal for Bobby Murcer. They paid Murcer more than what Madlock had asked for to re-sign.

That really bothered me. You hear so many Cubs fans complaining about the team not winning a championship for so many years, and that was a good example of why. The Cubs had an outstanding ballplayer in Madlock and they let him get away.

Wrigley, who was 82 years old at the time, said, "I didn't give the other guys multiyear contracts. Why should I give you one?"

Cubs management did not communicate well with players like Madlock. If there was something he was or wasn't doing off the field that bothered them, then Cubs management should have talked to him about it. Instead, they traded him away. Bill was more outspoken as a black man than Ernie and I were. But everybody can't be the same. And the times were changing as well.

On the final day of the 1976 Cubs season, Madlock had four hits against the Expos, improving his batting average six points to beat out Ken Griffey of the Reds for the batting title. Griffey had not started his final game, but entered after getting the word that Madlock had two hits. Griffey went 0-for-2 and finished at .336.

Pitching for the Master

People today talk about pitchers with great split-finger pitches. Well, Lindy McDaniel had a great one in my era. We usually called it a forkball back in those days. He was an effective pitcher for a long time. We used him more as a relief pitcher when he was with the Cubs, and he got some key outs for us when they really counted late in the game.

He was traded to the Cubs from the St. Louis Cardinals. Lindy was a born-again Christian and I remember that he always used to hand out pamphlets called "Pitching for the Master" to all of his teammates. He was a very religious guy.

But when he was with the Cardinals, the series between the Cubs and St. Louis were always heated and competitive. The fans got into those series, just as they do today. And so do the players. Anyway, one particular game I recall, McDaniel was pitching for the Cardinals and Ron Santo stood in the batter's box. The Cardinals were leading by a run and McDaniel fired a high hard one that almost hit Santo in the head.

Santo hit the dirt as his helmet flew off. As he got up and dusted himself off, Santo stared out at McDaniel and yelled, "Pitching for the Master, huh? I got your Pitching for the Master." Santo was really mad. But Lindy later said, "You have to do that sometimes. That is part of the game."

Santo replied, "You send me all of those pamphlets about pitching for the Master and you are trying to kill me."

Saluting the Flag

A number one draft choice out of Arizona State, Rick Monday had starred for the Dodgers before we got him in Chicago. I thought he played center field great for us.

Rick remains known for the time a protester came on the field in Los Angeles and tried to burn the American flag. Monday ran over and scooped up the flag before the protester could set it on fire. It was a spontaneous patriotic act that people in America will never forget. That is the kind of guy he is.

When he joined the Cubs, Rick would have parties at his house. He said that stemmed from his stint with the Dodgers. They always had social functions to bring the club closer together.

I recall one particular game when we were playing against San Diego and Pat Corrales was the Padres catcher. A pitch came in close to Monday and he and Corrales got into an argument. While they were arguing at home plate, Cardenal was yelling from our bench, "Watch him, he'll sucker punch you!"

Just as the words got out of Cardenal's mouth, Corrales hit Monday in the face and a big fight ensued. But Corrales never took off his catcher's mask so Monday couldn't retaliate the way he wanted.

Rick was the kind of guy who would hit 12 to 15 home runs for us. And he could run very well. He was a great defensive center fielder. Now he is announcing ballgames for the Dodgers and I talk to him every time I go to Los Angeles.

Rent Free

The Cubs signed Billy North, originally, and they brought him to the big leagues right away. There was a Major League

Baseball strike right after that but we wanted everybody to stay in Chicago.

Billy said, "Hey, I am just a rookie. I don't have enough money to stay in Chicago."

So Fergie Jenkins and I rented a place for him in Chicago because we didn't think there would be a strike for that long. In the meantime, we would all meet together on a certain day and work out.

It turned out that Fergie and I paid for Billy's apartment the whole year because we knew he was going to be a good ballplayer and a center fielder, which he was.

It turned out that Fergie and I paid for Billy's apartment the whole year because we knew he was going to be a good ballplayer and a center fielder, which he was. He was a good friend of Dusty Baker, and he always came to spring training to say hello.

Billy was the kind of guy who could be laughing one minute, and if you crossed him, he would be evil. That's what happened to him with Reggie Jackson in Oakland. That's why they went at it in Detroit. That was one of the reasons Ray Fosse hurt his shoulder. He had hurt his shoulder when Pete Rose collided with him at home plate in the All-Star Game. But he re-injured it over in Detroit when Billy North and Reggie Jackson fought for about 45 minutes. Billy was a tough little dude.

Nowadays he is living in Seattle. He always appreciated what Fergie and I did for him, renting that apartment for him in Chicago. He was a daredevil on the field, stealing bases and diving for balls in the outfield. In order to stay in the big leagues a long time, he made himself a switch-hitter after being a natural right-handed hitter. He played on those great Oakland teams in the 1970s, and he played great center field.

He Will Be Missed

Gene Oliver was a backup catcher for us on the 1969 Cubs team and everybody knows how many games Randy caught, so Gene mainly pinch-hit for us.

Gene was good at keeping everybody loose and relaxed on the bench and in the clubhouse. I remember one day in 1969 when we had a seven- or eight-game lead in August. Gene Oliver said at that time, "If we don't win the championship this year, I will jump off the John Hancock building downtown."

Our longtime clubhouse man, Yosh Kawano, overheard Oliver make this statement. At the end of the year, when we surrendered the lead to the New York Mets, Yosh turned to Oliver and said, "You still here?" Yosh used to tease him about that all the time.

But Gene kept everybody laughing. He also played with the Cardinals and Braves. With Atlanta, he used to be in that lineup with Hank Aaron, Rico Carty, and Eddie Mathews. They used to hit a lot of home runs. But whenever the Braves played the Los Angeles Dodgers and Sandy Koufax was pitching, Gene Oliver was in the lineup. That was because he was one of the guys Koufax couldn't get out. Everything Koufax would throw up there Oliver would hit. His claim to fame was always being in the lineup, hitting Koufax like he owned him.

God bless his soul, Gene Oliver just passed away in 2007. We were all out in Arizona at one of Randy Hundley's fantasy camps. As a matter of fact, it was the 25ᵗʰ anniversary of the camps. A lot of the players from the '69 team were out there. And we also celebrated Ernie Banks's 75ᵗʰ birthday.

Gene Oliver acted as the host of the campers, and at the banquet he was the emcee. We all noticed that he had become very hoarse, but we thought that just resulted from him talking so much. When we asked him what was wrong, he said he had developed some kind of ailment with his esophagus. When he got it checked out, it was determined he was going to need an operation. I talked to Gene on the phone and he said, "Everything is fine. I just have to go into the hospital and the doctors are going to do some work."

The next day I was told that he went in and they prepped him to perform the operation, but Gene started hemorrhaging and he passed away. It was so sad. We had all just spent time together the previous month in Chicago at the Cubs Convention. It was Gene and his wife, and Ron Santo and his wife, me and Shirley, and Beckert. We were all just sitting around and laughing and talking about old times. It was really shocking to learn that he had passed away. I knew that he had suffered a heart attack about a year or two beforehand, but his passing still was totally unexpected.

Still Seeking Perfection

Milt Pappas came over to the Cubs from Atlanta in 1970. He was really a gung-ho guy. In between pitches, he would hang his arms down like he was tired but, all of a sudden, he would gradually build up his momentum for the delivery to home plate. He had great control as a pitcher and he got a lot of hitters out with his slider.

He had pitched for Baltimore, Cincinnati, and Atlanta before joining the Cubs, where he twice won 17 games for us.

He was another pitcher who protected the hitters on the Cubs. In other words, if an opposing pitcher threw at us, Milt would say to us in the dugout, "Don't worry about it. I will get their guys." That's how the game was played back then. Leo Durocher wouldn't have to tell Milt to brush the hitters back, Milt would do it on his own.

When Milt first joined our ballclub, he decided to move to the western suburbs of Chicago, as I did with my family. Most of our teammates lived in the northern suburbs. So Milt and I often would ride back and forth to the ballpark. We used to have great conversations. I also used to do some bird hunting out that way with him. We got to know each other real well.

Of course, Milt Pappas will always be known for pitching a no-hitter against the San Diego Padres in 1972. It would have been a perfect game, but home-plate umpire Bruce Froemming called a close 3–2 pitch a ball with two outs in the ninth inning to ruin it.

I have seen that close pitch given to a lot of pitchers when they are pitching a great game. Bruce, who was a young guy then, called it a ball. I think any other guy would have called it a different way. But I think that because Bruce was coming into the league, he wanted to do everything by the book and he called it a ball. Milt started walking off the mound and I think he called Froemming every name under the sun. Because that could have been a perfect game, and there have not been that many perfect games. Every now and then Milt will talk about that game and he gets red in the face when he does.

The 1972 season was the best of Pappas's career. He won 17 games to tie his career high, he pitched a no-hitter, and he won his 200th career game.

He finished his career in 1973 with a sore arm when he was 34. But he wound up with more than 200 wins.

Can I Borrow Your Hair Dryer?

When Joe Pepitone came to the Cubs in Chicago, I think he had two or three ex-wives coming after him. I never thought he would settle down, but he finally married a girl named Stevie, whom he is still with. When I see him every year in Arizona, he still talks about her. But Joe has gone through a whole lot. He is one guy who was able to convince me to go fishing on a Sunday. I had never fished on Sundays before, but he convinced me to go with him.

When Joe came here to Chicago, Leo Durocher was the manager. Houston had gotten rid of Pepitone for some reason and Leo decided to take him for the Cubs in 1970. Joe had previously played for the Yankees for eight seasons and had developed quite a reputation as a flamboyant late-night carouser. He used to run around with Mickey Mantle in New York and they got into a lot of mischief.

Joe was always an outstanding ballplayer; it was just a matter of him concentrating on playing the game of baseball. He hit more than 200 homers during his 12 seasons in the big leagues. When Pepitone first came to the Cubs, Leo went to John Holland and got Joe $25,000 to pay off some of his ex-wives. Otherwise, he couldn't concentrate on playing ball. Every time he did something, one of the ex-wives would be calling to bother him. When he got his first check, he might have gotten two dollars and 99 cents after the rest of the money went to different wives.

But the night after Leo had given him the $25,000 to pay off his ex-wives, a bunch of us went over to a clothing store in Cincinnati called Geno's. Joe ordered two suits, a couple sport coats, and a bunch of other clothes. He was a real sharp dresser. He brought them into the clubhouse and Leo saw him and just went wild, calling him all kind of names. "I just bailed you out with your ex-wives and then you go out and spend a ton of money like that. How could you do that?"

We didn't know Pepitone that well personally when he first joined our ballclub. But I remember one time in Cincinnati, he was the first player on our team to bring a hair dryer into the clubhouse. And he was always the last guy to leave the clubhouse because he didn't want anybody else to know that he had this toupee he was wearing. I happened to be one of the last guys to leave the clubhouse in Cincinnati that particular night.

I was in the bathroom and overheard this sound of a hair dryer. I had never heard that sound in the clubhouse before. I looked over and saw that Joe was drying his toupee, which he later called his "night life." Not too many people saw him without his toupee on. He never did take his helmet off when he was batting. When I saw his toupee in the clubhouse, he was kind of surprised because he didn't want anybody to know.

But Leo always treated Pepitone as if he was his own son. He really liked him. Leo loved Pepitone and he loved Beckert. That's because Beckert was a guy who reminded him of Eddie Stanky. He was that kind of player. The rest of us on the club could do something wrong and get in trouble, but when Beckert did something, we all thought he could get away clean. It was the same way with Pepitone.

Pepitone would always come to the ballpark in this limo and had the driver set out a red carpet for him to walk on to the ballpark. He also owned this chopper motorcycle, and he would get our clubhouse man, Yosh

Joe just didn't concentrate on baseball like other players. His focus was more on what was happening after the game.

Kawano, to open up the door of the clubhouse. Then Joe would ride the chopper between Leo and his desk in his office. A lot of times Leo would just slam the door and tell Yosh, "Get that damn thing outta here." But that's where Joe parked it every day.

Joe just didn't concentrate on baseball like other players. His focus was more on what was happening after the game. Everybody knew Pepitone in Chicago. He opened a club called The Thing. That's where a lot of guys on the team would go when he first opened the place. We all went over there to support him. It was a place where a lot of young people would hang out. It was a lot of fun. He didn't have that place for very long. But he was a likable guy.

I still see him every year out in Arizona. I tell you, this guy could be a comedian. All of the players and ex-players still have a lot of fun with him. He enjoys life.

The Next Willie Mays
Adolfo Phillips was dubbed "The Panamanian Flash" when he first came over to our ballclub from Philadelphia in the

trade with Fergie Jenkins and John Herrnstein in 1966. The Cubs sent Bob Buhl and Larry Jackson to the Phillies.

In 1966, Leo Durocher told everybody that Phillips could become the next Willie Mays. And I thought that was going to be the case, too, because he had all the tools to be such a great player. He hit the ball for high average, he hit the balls in the gap, and he could run really well in the outfield and on the bases. He even stole home for us one time in a game against the Mets.

But Adolfo's temperament seemed to work against him. He thought everybody was picking on him all of the time. That's the kind of guy he was. I would try to be friends with him to get him to relax. As ballplayers, we would receive watches or radios for being guests on pregame radio shows. Just to make Phillips feel welcome on the ballclub, I would give him a radio or a watch after I had been interviewed.

Phillips was a good ballplayer, and one day during a doubleheader against the Mets at Wrigley Field, he hit four home runs, three of them in consecutive at-bats in the second game. He had six hits and eight RBIs that day. He was just a tremendous talent.

But the next couple of games, pitchers brushed him back and threw some balls near his head. It seems to me that after that Adolfo didn't seem to have the heart to stay in position to drive the ball the way he once did. That was the kind of test that most major league pitchers will put you through after you hit a few home runs, especially during that era. If you struggle a little bit after those brushbacks, then the pitchers will continue to do that. They know that they have intimidated you as a hitter.

Phillips hit 16 homers his first year with the Cubs and 17 in 1967. But he hit just 13 in his final year in Chicago. He refused to bat leadoff, to take advantage of his speed, and Durocher became increasingly frustrated with him.

Phillips started striking out a lot more and struggling at the plate. He struck out 135 times in just 116 games in 1966. Durocher traded Phillips away three years later to Montreal and then called him the most disappointing player he had ever managed.

The Vulture Strikes Again

We used to call Phil Regan "The Vulture" because he would come into the game so many times as a reliever when we were trailing. But we would rally late in the game and he would be credited with the victory.

He came over to the Cubs from the Dodgers and they actually gave him that nickname because he collected a lot of victories the same way in Los Angeles. You talk about a competitor! Regan and Ron Santo were two of the best competitors on the ballclub. They wanted to win at all costs.

A lot of people accused him of throwing illegal pitches, saying that he would wet one up for a spitter and stuff like that. But he wanted to win.

Even when we were playing charity basketball games in the winter months, Regan would come down from his home in Michigan to play. From time to time things would get rough on the basketball court. Regan wanted to fight a couple of guys in those charity games because he wanted to win so badly.

One time, at a Fantasy Baseball Camp, there was a simulated game created between the 1969 Cubs and Mets. Former

Mets outfielder Ron Swoboda was on the microphone and said something like, "How are the Cubs going to be able to beat the Mets this time?" Regan got real mad when he heard that and challenged Swoboda to a fight at one of those camps. He was some kind of competitor.

A Wicked Cricket Player

One of the few big-league ballplayers from Nassau, Bahamas, Andre Rodgers had been a good cricket player back in his homeland. You could tell that when he played baseball because he was a good low-ball hitter. And he used to explain the game of cricket to me.

When he came over to the Cubs from San Francisco in 1961, Andre was a shortstop. That's when Ernie Banks had made the shift from short to first base. Actually, Andre had been traded from the Giants to the Milwaukee Braves following the 1960 season. But he never played for the Braves because they sent him to the Cubs in the spring of '61 in exchange for pitchers Moe Drabowsky and Seth Morehead.

Andre had a daughter by the name of Gina, I believe, and, of course, Shirley and I had two or three daughters at the time so our families got along well. I made several trips to Nassau to visit Andre and he came to visit us in Mobile. We would drive from Mobile to spring training in Arizona together. That's how we got to know each other really well.

The housing for us during spring training in Mesa, Arizona, wasn't that good at the time. Andre's wife, Eunice, used to cook breakfast for us during spring training before we would go to the ballpark.

Andre was a terrific shortstop, but he had some problems in Chicago after he made a couple of mistakes in the field.

People started booing him at Wrigley Field and I think that kind of destroyed him. He didn't take it well.

After the games, Andre loved to drink his beer. He was a big beer drinker. Even when he was out of baseball and back in the Bahamas all he would do was drink beer and lay out on the beach. When I first started going out to the Bahamas to visit him, Andre had a nice sporting goods shop where he sold all kinds of tennis equipment.

Andre was a terrific short-stop, but he had some problems in Chicago after he made a couple of mistakes in the field.

One time when I went to visit Andre in the Bahamas, the reclusive Howard Hughes occupied the entire ninth floor of the hotel where I was staying. I didn't get a chance to see him that much because nobody else was allowed on the ninth floor. But Hughes's entire family was there, and they would go to Andre's shop to buy tennis equipment.

Andre was a good guy and we enjoyed each other. He passed away in the Bahamas in 2004 at the age of 70. His wife came back to the United States after that and she and my wife remain good friends.

A Symbol of Perseverance

I think I knew Ronnie Santo better than most people when we were playing ball together. There could be 49,000 people in the stands and 48,999 of them could be cheering for him and the Cubs. But Ronnie would hear that one guy booing. That's the way he was. He was a competitor who didn't like to lose. He wanted to win at all costs. And I have seen him get in scrapes and holler at guys. That was just his temperament.

We came up through the minors and into the big leagues together. I remember that Ronnie signed a big-league contract in 1959 and, back in those days, we called the players signed right out of high school "bonus babies" or "high school Harrys." Ronnie came down to spring training in Arizona driving his fancy Chevy Impala.

Ronnie and I hit it off right away and became friends because we knew each other in Class AA baseball. Baseball observers always seemed to talk about my progression and Ronnie's progression in the same sentences. He was a catcher before he became a third baseman.

Rogers Hornsby, a Hall of Fame ballplayer and then a batting instructor for the Cubs, came down there to the minors and kind of took Ronnie and me under his wing.

While in the minors in the Texas League, I remember Ronnie and I

There could be 49,000 people in the stands and 48,999 of them could be cheering for him and the Cubs. But Ronnie would hear that one guy booing.

had to go Mexico for nine days to play games in the Pan American League. Ronnie, J.C. Hartman, and I saw this swimming pool next to our motel with no water in it. Of course, the weather was so unbelievably hot in Mexico in the summer. We snuck a water hose in there and filled it up. Later that night, following the baseball game, we went back around midnight and dove off our room balconies into the pool, just to cool off.

To this day, Ronnie absolutely detests the New York Mets. In fact, I don't think he even likes being in the city of New York. I remember that on September 9, 1969, we received a bad omen in New York. A black cat came out on the field when we played the Mets at Shea Stadium. The cat walked around Santo, who was standing in the on-deck circle. The cat then came toward our dugout and sort of made a hissing sound at Durocher. We lost that game to Tom Seaver and the Mets and our downward spiral continued.

To this day, Ronnie absolutely detests the New York Mets. In fact, I don't think he even likes being in the city of New York.

Ronnie had a great career with the Cubs as a Gold Glove third baseman and an outstanding hitter. I have even greater respect for him today, knowing what he had to go through to achieve those great stats.

I had no idea that Ronnie was a diabetic when he played. He kept it a secret. Our trainer back then had a little black pouch. When it was hot during the summer, he would place that pouch on the dugout bench and he would store a lot of Hershey chocolate bars in there. We didn't know that they were for Santo. So guys like Glenn Beckert and I would go in there and eat up all of those candy bars.

I give him a lot of credit for what he was able to accomplish on the field.

Beckert and Santo roomed together on the road for years. One time Beckert happened to open the bathroom door and saw Santo injecting himself with a needle. Now, at the time, Santo was hitting about .325 and Beckert was hitting under .200. Beckert must have thought Santo was injecting himself with some type of performance enhancer,

126

so he said, "Hey, man. Is that why you're hitting so well? Give me some of that."

Beckert later found out that Ronnie was a diabetic, and he helped Santo keep his secret from his teammates and the public. Nowadays, Santo does a tremendous job with the Juvenile Diabetes Research Foundation.

Savage Attack

Ted Savage used to stay at the Executive House hotel in Chicago when he played with the Cubs, and I would routinely drop him off there after games at Wrigley Field.

Leo Durocher always used to tell the team that his office door was open. He would say, "If you have any beef, I want you to come talk to me." But Savage would never do that. Ted would always complain to me and say, "Billy, go talk to Leo. I want to play more."

But Ted was kind of intimidated by Leo. At that time we also had Lee Thomas playing the outfield. Thomas would become the general manager for St. Louis.

Leo was the kind of guy who could make you laugh. But he could also say some things that dug deep. One time we were losing in the late innings of a game, and Leo told Lee Thomas to grab a bat to pinch hit. I happened to be sitting next to Leo on the bench at the time. Leo said, "I don't know why I sent him up there. He can't catch, he can't hit the ball. He can't do anything. Watch him pop up."

Sure enough, Lee Thomas popped out and Leo said, "I told you, I told you."

Leo looked over at Savage, who was sitting on the bench. At that point we had lost five or six games in a row. Leo said, "Savage, go down and sit in the bullpen. You're bad luck."

In truth, Savage was a good outfielder who could run really well. When he played in our charity basketball games during the off-season, you could tell he had tremendous athletic ability. It seemed like he could jump out of the arena. He was an outstanding basketball player. He didn't get a chance to play that much on the Cubs, but when he did, he did pretty well.

Now Savage is in the corporate marketing business in St. Louis and he is doing a great job.

A Left-Handed Complement

Sammy Taylor was a left-handed-hitting catcher for us. He would alternate with Moe Thacker, who was a right-handed-hitting catcher.

The Cubs acquired him from the Milwaukee Braves, along with Taylor Phillips, before the 1958 season for Bob Rush, Don Kaiser, and Eddie Haas.

I think that Sammy was one of those guys who emphasized hitting more than catching. He got some big hits for us and hit 13 homers in 1959, his best season offensively.

I don't remember Taylor as being a real good defensive catcher. In fact, he had 10 errors and six passed balls in 1959. But he could really pull the ball as a hitter. When the New York Mets became an expansion team in 1962, Sammy became a part of that club following a trade for Bobby Gene Smith. He finished up his career with brief stints with the Reds and Indians.

Tony Taylor

I remember riding in Tony's Chevy Impala back when I was just a young player. I thought that car was great, and

I said, "I might want one of these when I can afford it later in my career."

Tony was the second baseman and we really enjoyed each other's company. We would have lunch together before we went to the ballpark. At the end of the year, I knew he was going back to Cuba. So I drove back to Valdosta, Georgia, with him while he slept. From that point Tony went to Miami to catch a flight to Cuba.

I watched a movie in a theater in Valdosta until it was time for me to catch a bus to Mobile, Alabama.

Tony and Ernie Banks formed a great double-play combination when Ernie was the shortstop. A lot of people were unhappy when Lou Boudreau came down from the broadcast booth to take over for Charlie Grimm as manager. Boudreau had Tony traded to Philadelphia in 1960 along with Cal Neeman in exchange for Don Cardwell and Ed Bouchee. I think that trade hurt Ernie's feelings a little bit. Tony also was a leadoff hitter who could move the ball around to all fields. He handled the bat well for the hit-and-run, and he was an excellent bunter.

I remember that every time Tony came to bat he would give himself the sign of the cross and close his eyes. The fans in Philadelphia really loved Tony. He stole home six times as a member of the Phillies. He later played three years for the Detroit Tigers before finishing up his career back with the Phillies. He wound up with more than 2,000 hits. He has been a coach for the Phillies for several years.

Overcoming Tragedy

I got to know Andre Thornton very well when he played first base for the Cubs in 1973. He was driving to his hometown of Philadelphia with his family in 1977 to attend a wedding. Thornton's van spun out of control when it hit a patch of ice on the mountain road near Somerset, Pennsylvania. His vehicle crashed into a guardrail and turned over, killing his wife, Gert, and three-year-old daughter, Theresa. Andre and his four-year-old son, Andy, survived the crash. Andre went through a lot of bereavement following that, and I used to talk to him from time to time.

A lot of people don't know that he was an outstanding pool player. Andre once told me that when he was growing up in Philadelphia he would get a lot of sucker bets by missing a few shots on purpose while playing in front of a group of guys. Andre made a lot of money doing that while growing up in Philly.

That was in great contrast to his life now, because he is a minister in Cleveland, Ohio. The people love him over in Cleveland because when the Cubs traded him there in 1977 he became a two-time All-Star and three times hit more than 30 homers.

Andre has been a good guy in the community in Cleveland. A few years ago, when the Cubs were in the National League playoffs, I got him tickets to the game and we sat behind the third-base dugout at Wrigley Field. His son, Andy, attended Wheaton College in the western suburbs of Chicago. I would talk to Andy occasionally just to let him know that he has a friend here in Chicago.

Where There is a Will, There is a Way

My competition with the Cubs to become the starting left fielder in 1961 was veteran Bob Will. When I first came up to the big leagues, I wasn't swinging the bat real well. I envied Bob Will and I told him, "This is my position."

Bob was a good, solid ballplayer, but he did not hit for much power.

But I sat on the bench at first and said to myself, "When I get back in the lineup, nobody is going to take me out." Bob started for about two weeks as I sat on the bench and tried to recognize what I was doing wrong. Eventually, Bob Will came up with a bad neck. So I was in the lineup the next day. From that point on, I found myself hitting the ball really well in the big leagues.

But I sat on the bench at first and said to myself, "When I get back in the lineup, nobody is going to take me out."

That competition with Bob Will was the first determining factor in whether I would make it in the big leagues. Bob remained on the team as a backup outfielder and he was our appointed team representative.

My relationship with Bob was good, even though I took his position. He knew that I had had some good years in the minor leagues and that many people had projected that I would become the starting left fielder in 1961. Bob Will had succeeded Walt Moryn in left field and then I took over for Will.

Bob was born in Berwyn, Illinois, and broke into the big leagues in 1957 when he was 25 years old, after attending Northwestern University. He played a couple more years with the Cubs after I became a starter, then retired in 1963.

An Oscar Performance

Oscar Zamora looked like he was going to be a good pitcher when he first joined the Cubs in 1974, but he struggled, I believe, with some off-the-field issues. His record was only 3–9 the first year he joined our ballclub, which happened to be my last season with the Cubs. He did have 10 saves as he contributed as a reliever.

"Zim" was known as a scrappy ballplayer who would do whatever he could to beat the opponent.

Oscar was 29 when made his big-league debut. He was born in Cuba and attended Miami Dade College. Zamora's claim to fame probably came in the minor leagues when he pitched a perfect game for the Oklahoma City 89ers against the Denver Bears in 1972.

He had a better season in 1975, finishing with a 5–2 record. But his big-league career lasted only four years, ending in Houston. I will just remember the promise of a fine career that he showed when he first joined our ballclub, and I know timing can be very important in sports and in life. In 1974 the Cubs were going through a transition of sorts, getting rid of some veteran players like me and trying to bring in some new faces.

Oscar was one of only four players born in Cuba who made their debut in the majors during the 1970s.

A Head of the Times

Although he was a member of the Cubs when I first joined the team in 1961, I really didn't get the opportunity to know Don Zimmer as well as I did later when he became a coach and then the manager of the Cubs.

"Zim" was known as a scrappy ballplayer who would do whatever he could to beat the opponent.

The Cubs had acquired Zimmer from the Dodgers early in the 1960 season in return for infielder Johnny Goryl, outfielder Lee Handley, minor league pitcher Ron Perranoski, and cash. Perranoski (who I roomed with in 1967) would emerge as the top reliever in the National League.

Zimmer batted .252 with 13 homers in 1961, but he went to the Mets in the October 1961 expansion draft.

Even though I did not get a chance to really know Zimmer when we were teammates in 1961, all of us had heard the story that he had a metal plate in his head.

In 1953, I guess Zimmer was leading the American Association with 23 home runs and 63 runs batted in when he was hit on the head by a pitch from a minor league pitcher named Jim Kirk.

Zimmer was unconscious for nearly two weeks. He lost his ability to speak for six weeks and lost 44 pounds. At that point, doctors inserted what Zimmer later described as four "buttons that looked like tapered corkscrews in a bottle." Somehow, Zimmer returned to baseball in 1954 and was the Brooklyn Dodgers' second baseman in the 1955 World Series. But in 1956 another pitch—this time from Cincinnati's Hal Jeffcoat—fractured Zimmer's cheekbone and ended that season for him.

Still, Zimmer would not be denied. He was the Dodgers' starting shortstop in 1958. In 1959 he lost his job to Maury Wills as the Dodgers defeated the Chicago White Sox in the World Series.

CHAPTER 5

That Sweet Swing

The longest home run that I can recall hitting for the Chicago Cubs came against Ron Herbel of the San Francisco Giants back in the mid-1960s. The ball cleared the right-field bleachers at Wrigley Field and landed across Sheffield Avenue, breaking a window in an apartment building. They weren't able to calculate the actual distance of home runs back in those days. And, to tell you the truth, I always let other people worry about how far my home runs went. The most important thing to me was just having the ball clear the fence. You don't get credit for more than one run if you hit it 500 feet.

I had a lot of success against Herbel during my career. He was a pretty decent right-hander, finishing his career with more wins than losses (42–37). I was more proud of the fact that I hit well against Hall of Fame flame-thrower Bob Gibson, one of the most feared and dominating pitchers of all time.

Gibson was a very competitive pitcher, and I guess he thought he could get me out on a pitch that was down and in. But when he threw it there he really was playing to my strength and power all of those years. I loved to swing at pitches down and in. I wound up hitting 11 career homers off Gibson, including a couple of game-winners. That was unheard of against him. It was a case of me being an aggressive hitter and Bob being an aggressive pitcher.

I had been given the nickname "Sweet Swinging" Billy Williams long before that memorable long blast. A sportswriter back in Class AA San Antonio stuck that nickname on me. Even though I weighed only about 173 pounds during most of my playing career, I was always able to generate enough bat speed and leverage to hit for power.

> **I generally hit my balls on a line, and that gave me an opportunity to hit more home runs, regardless of the wind conditions.**

When a hitter tries to pull the ball all of the time, too many holes are developed in the swing. I generally hit my balls on a line, and that gave me an opportunity to hit more home runs, regardless of the wind conditions. So many people consider Wrigley Field to be a hitter's ballpark because of the favorable dimensions. But the wind blows in more often than it blows out at Wrigley. I didn't try to pull everything that came up to me on the plate. I didn't want to over-swing and fall into that temptation. I just tried to hit the ball hard.

Richie Ashburn, who was a veteran outfield teammate of mine when I first joined the Cubs, noticed that I had a slight hitch in my swing. But he expressed confidence that I would be able to hit in the big leagues.

I always felt that my swing came naturally. It was not altered or tinkered with to any great extent by any batting coach or manager. I was blessed in that respect. The key to my swing was to make it quick and get the bat head on the ball. Simple as that. When I was in the minor leagues at San Antonio, Rogers Hornsby agreed that when I held my bat straight up and perpendicular to the ground, I could wait on the ball a split second longer before committing to the pitch.

Many times it would appear that I was able to hit the ball out of the catcher's mitt, that's how long I was able to wait on a pitch. I generally used a 32-ounce, 34-and-one-half inch model bat. On occasion I would go to a 31-ounce bat. And I always preferred the wide-grain bats. The quality of the wood bats today is not nearly as good as the ones we had.

Our clubhouse man, Yosh Kawano, would make certain I had top-quality bats available for my use, even from the first time I appeared in the big leagues in 1959. Yosh said, "Son, it's best we get along, because I think we are going to be together for a long time."

He was right. I was with the Cubs for 16 years.

Because there are so many different companies making wooden bats today, it seems that a lot of them are poorly made. Go to any Major League Baseball game now and you will witness at least two or three bats exploding on contact with the baseball. The barrel of the bat might fly out on the playing field and hit an opposing player. Or, even scarier than that, the bat might go flying into the stands and seriously injure a fan. That's a part of the action that a fan does not want to see up close.

In Little League, high school, and college baseball nowadays, the batters use aluminum bats to save on the cost of replacing broken and splintered wood bats. But that creates another set of problems. First of all, big-league scouts have a tougher time evaluating the younger talent using the aluminum bats. Many of the base hits they are able to muscle into the outfield off the handle of the bats at the lower levels would be broken-bat outs with the wood bats in the big leagues. That makes it difficult to evaluate young hitters and young pitchers.

From the time I hit my first big-league home run off Stan Williams of the Dodgers in the Los Angeles Memorial Coliseum on October 1, 1960, I took great pride in my bats and considered them my weapons of choice, if you will, when it came to defending myself against lethal major league pitchers such as Sandy Koufax, Warren Spahn, Don Drysdale, and Gibson.

I always felt that my swing came naturally. It was not altered or tinkered with to any great extent by any batting coach or manager. I was blessed in that respect.

I made my major league debut on August 6, 1959. We beat the Phillies 4–2 that day. I hit .152 that year, getting only 33 at-bats. In 1960, I improved to .277 in 47 at-bats.

When we went on the road, Yosh would bring five or six of my favorite bats for me and put them in the bat rack. Yosh would call the people at Louisville Slugger to order my new bats throughout the year. When he would call them and say that he wanted some bats for Billy Williams, they would know right away just what kind I wanted. They were always the same.

One time Yosh called me to tell me that my new bats had arrived. So, before the next game, I took a look at the new bats. I was a big believer in the wide-grain bats. When a player on a team is swinging the bat well, a lot of the other players want to use his bat. So I would tell Yosh, "When another player asks to use one of my bats, don't give him one of my wide-grained bats in the trunk in the back of the clubhouse. Give him one of the other ones."

After using the same kind of bat for a long time like I did, you have a good feel for it and you know the weight of the bat. And you know how the weight was distributed. One time Yosh called the folks at Louisville Slugger and they sent the wrong bats. On the bat it read that they were 32-ounce bats, but they did not feel right to me.

I said, "Yosh, they sent me the wrong order."

Yosh said, "No, on the bat it says '32 ounces.'"

I said, "I don't care what it says on the bat, this is not a 32-ounce bat."

So I asked Yosh to take the bats

Before I had two strikes on me, I would swing hard and really try to drive the ball.

to the post office to have them weighed. Sure enough, the bats were more than 33 ounces each. So he took the bats and sent them back to Louisville. Plus, I wanted the handle a little bit smaller.

Back when I played, there were only five or six different bat models. But now, the players have so many different bat models in their lockers that they can't get comfortable with one of them.

I was known as a good two-strike hitter in my day. I might guess on a pitch when I had no strikes or one strike on me—but never with two strikes. You have to watch the pitch carefully with two strikes and then make a split-second adjustment.

Before I had two strikes on me, I would swing hard and really try to drive the ball. If we needed a home run, I would try to hit the ball out of the ballpark. That was my chance at a big swing. With one strike on me, I might try to do the same thing, but if there is a base runner on first base, I would pull the ball into the hole. With two strikes on me, my mentality was like a hockey goalie. I was protecting the plate at that time.

I never wanted to know ahead of time what pitch was going to be thrown because I was concerned that there might be a mistake in relaying the information to me. My first full year in the big leagues I got hit in the head with a pitch. When a young player comes to the big leagues, the veterans always test you to see what kind of reaction you will have to being hit. We were playing Cincinnati in 1961 and left-hander Jim O'Toole was pitching for the Reds. He had a little cut fastball. He started me off by pitching away and got a strike or two on the corner. Then he came inside with a fastball aimed at my head. We didn't have the batting helmets at the time; we just had the leather inserts that fit inside our caps.

> **It can be a helpless feeling to stand in the batter's box and see a fastball coming right at your head. You often do not have enough time to react.**

The fastball hit me in the head and I went down. The trainers took me to the hospital, and everything checked out okay. I believe the quicker you get back in the lineup and get that behind you, the better off you are. That is what I did the next day. I was ready to challenge the pitcher again. I wanted to get back in the lineup to let O'Toole know that I was not afraid, even though he hit me. From that point on, I always challenged O'Toole as a hitter.

It can be a helpless feeling to stand in the batter's box and see a fastball coming right at your head. You often do not have enough time to react. I have talked to many pitchers over the years and they have told me that if a major league pitcher wants to hit a batter on the head with a pitch, he can do it. A pitcher can throw a fastball behind you and the first instinct for a hitter is to lean backwards. If you don't pick up the ball from the pitcher's hand, your first move is to go back. That's where the pitcher aims when he really wants to hit you. But that used to be part of the game.

If you hit a home run, next time you came up to the plate, the pitchers wanted to see what the heck you were made of. They would throw the ball inside and brush you back a little bit.

I struck out 1,046 times in 9,350 at-bats during my 18-year career and hit 426 homers.

In the 1960s and early '70s, most of the pitchers had maybe four pitches they could throw: fastball, slider, curveball, and change-up. I figured that if I guessed wrong, the pitcher could get me out. So I tried not to guess. I tried to wait back, see the ball a little longer, and shorten my swing up. I just tried to meet the ball at that point. Striking out was a big thing to me. I didn't want to strike out.

I would go to the plate about 600 times a year for seven straight years, and I would strike out about 60 or 70 times a year. That was unheard of for a hitter like me who could drive the ball and hit 35 home runs a year. That was a rarity.

I struck out 1,046 times in 9,350 at-bats during my 18-year career and hit 426 homers. By comparison, Mickey Mantle was a terrific power hitter with 536 homers. He also played 18 seasons and he struck out 1,710 times in fewer (8,102) at-bats.

Ever since the game of baseball has been played professionally, players have tried to steal signs from the opposing catcher. Some of their methods have been pretty sophisticated. In a lot of ballparks, the home team batters would step into the batter's box and glance quickly out at the scoreboard after the catcher gave the sign to the pitcher. Maybe a light would flash once for a fastball or two times for a curve, something like that. Or if you were the

I will never forget that moment, subbing for Stan "The Man" Musial. What an honor!

batter and you had a teammate on second base looking in at the catcher's sign, there would be a way to relay the sign to the batter. A long time ago, I think they had something in the Wrigley Field scoreboard for the batters to look at. At Milwaukee County Stadium, there was a guy who used to wave a towel near the scoreboard to tip off the pitches to the Braves hitters.

There was always gamesmanship involved as teams tried to find ways to win. Maybe the base runner would use a crossover step while he was leading off to indicate a breaking pitch was on its way. Or he might tip his cap or give some other indicator. If one of the coaches was able to steal a sign or get a sense of the location of an upcoming pitch, he might bend over to let a hitter know the pitch was going to be on the outside part of the plate, or whatever.

I won the National League Rookie of the Year award in 1961, even though all of the talk much of that season was that Willie Davis of the Los Angeles Dodgers was going to win it. The 25 home runs I hit in 1961 is still a Cubs rookie record. In 1962, the late Ken Hubbs was named NL Rookie of the Year, giving the Cubs the award two straight years.

Davis had 12 homers and 12 stolen bases while hitting .254 for the Dodgers in 1961. He would go on to have an excellent career. His speed on the base paths made him quite a threat. He wound up his career with almost 400 stolen bases.

People wondered if the so-called "sophomore jinx" would hit me in 1962. But I put up solid numbers again: .298 batting average, 22 homers, and 91 RBIs. The second All-Star Game was held in Chicago that year, and I wanted to make certain I would be a member of that squad. I remember that legendary Reds manager Fred Hutchinson was the National League manager for that game at Wrigley Field. I was sitting on the bench during the game and Hutchinson yelled down to me, "Hey, Williams, go out in left field and pick up Musial."

I will never forget that moment, subbing for Stan "The Man" Musial. What an honor! I played in six All-Star Games and each time was very special for me. We lost that All-Star Game 9–4 to the American League, but I did manage to drive in a run. From 1959 to 1962, there were two All-Star Games played each year. The National League won the other game in 1962, by the score of 3–1, in Washington, D.C.

The second All-Star Game during that short span was designed to raise money for the players' pensions. But having two games sort of diluted the appeal of the game, and they went back to one All-Star Game in 1963.

I was always leery of somebody taking my job, especially early in my career. I guess that is what kept me going at full tilt all of the time. It might have also been the reason I played in 1,117 straight games from 1963 through 1970, which was then a league record. Steve Garvey broke that record in 1983. I guess I had a bit of an ego as far as not wanting anyone to take my place in left field. But most outstanding athletes in any sport thrive by having a big ego.

I sat out a game against the Braves on September 21, 1963. Warren Spahn, a tough Hall of Fame lefty, was the starting pitcher that game. Bob Kennedy decided to give me a rest. But the next day I began the consecutive game streak that lasted until September 2, 1970. If I had not sat out that game, my record streak would have been 1,283 games. Oh well.

I played in at least 150 games for 12 straight seasons, 1962–1973. Santo and I share the Cubs record for games in a season, 164. That is because there were two tie games replayed in 1965.

One of the most historic games I participated in during my career was one in which my so-called sweet swing was not so sweet. Sandy Koufax handcuffed all of us by pitching a perfect game on September 9, 1965, in Los Angeles. Bob Hendley pitched a heck of a game for us as well, allowing just one hit by Lou Johnson in the fifth inning.

Koufax struck out 14 while facing the minimum of batters, and he claimed me among his strikeout victims. In the first inning Don Kessinger led off and popped out. Then Beckert struck out against Koufax. Beckert was one of the hardest guys to strike out on our team. He would only fan about 25 times a year in 500 or 600 at-bats. I was in the on-deck circle and our cleanup hitter, Santo, was coming out of the dugout to bat behind me. As Beckert walked with his head down back to the dugout, Santo passed him going toward the on-deck circle.

"What's he got?" asked Santo.

"We should get him tonight. He ain't got shit," said Beckert.

The first at-bat I had against Koufax, I felt, was pivotal in the game. I remember it as if it was yesterday. The count was full against me. Koufax rared back and fired a fastball inside. I took the pitch, and I had a pretty good eye at the plate. The home-plate umpire that night was Ed Vargo, and he called it a strike. Vargo must have sensed that Koufax was going to throw a perfect game that night because I still think that pitch was inside.

But Koufax was throwing the ball really well that night, and we didn't have a chance up there. I remember Harvey Kuenn, a 34-year-old veteran that we had picked up from the Detroit Tigers, went to the plate as a pinch-hitter in the ninth inning. Joey Amalfitano, who had pinch-hit earlier in that game, said in the dugout, "I don't know why they are sending that guy up to the plate, the way Koufax is throwing tonight."

Koufax proceeded to strike out Kuenn to end the perfect game and the Dodgers won 1–0.

Koufax had a dominant fastball that night. And he had a devastating curve. When he got both of those pitches over, you had no chance. Those were the only pitches he had—fastball and curveball.

When the Dodgers were playing Minnesota in the 1965 World Series, Koufax was pitching on just two days' rest and he couldn't get his curveball over the plate.

Johnny Roseboro, the Dodgers catcher, went to the mound early in that game and said to Koufax, "What the hell are you throwing today?"

Koufax said, "I can't get my curveball over today."

Then Koufax told Roseboro, "Look, whatever signs you put down for me to throw the rest of the game, don't look for anything but a fastball. That's all I am throwing today."

Koufax wound up throwing a three-hit, 2–0 victory with 10 strikeouts. Over the course of his brief career, Koufax threw four no-hitters. Severe arthritis in his left elbow ended his career in 1966.

But I found that if I waited long enough and made them throw me a lot of pitches, at some point I would get a pitch that looked like it was sitting on a tee.

The perfect game he threw against us in 1965 was a tough loss, and the atmosphere in Dodger Stadium that night was like a playoff game. There were more than 29,000 fans there and most of them stayed until the very end. Usually, Dodgers fans arrive late and leave early to avoid the traffic. But not this particular night. The people didn't want to miss a perfect game.

Lou Klein was our Cubs manager in 1965. After a game like that, you feel bad about Koufax throwing a perfect game against you. But after we sat in the clubhouse a while, we tipped our hats to Koufax. We just took our showers and tried to come out the next day and get them.

The only pitcher in today's game who comes close to Koufax as a dominant left-hander with electric stuff would be Johan Santana of the Twins. He struck out 17 batters in a game in 2007. Santana has a great change-up too. That is a pitch Koufax never had.

My most productive offensive seasons came in 1970 and '72. In 1970, I batted .322 with 42 homers and 129 RBIs.

Even though we wound up relinquishing the division lead to the Mets, everybody on the Cubs felt pretty good going into the 1970 season. For me, it all started out well in spring training. I wanted to have about two at-bats a game early in spring training. Then, toward the end of spring training, I wanted at least three at-bats a game. That helped me get ready for the regular season.

I started off the 1970 season well, driving the ball to all fields. I was just seeing the ball well. And right up until the final couple weeks of the season, I was hitting a lot of home runs. I wound up with 42 at the end of the season.

One of the constant debates in baseball is whether the baseball is wound tighter in certain years, creating a livelier ball that is more likely to be hit out of the ballpark. In my estimation, it just depends from year to year whether the pitchers are doing a better job of getting the hitters out. I never noticed any significant difference in the quality of the baseballs.

We won 84 games in 1970 and finished in second place. Jim Hickman also had an outstanding year in 1970, hitting .315 with 32 homers. Hickman, Beckert, and Kessinger joined me on the NL All-Star team that year.

In 1972 I won the National League batting title with a .333 average. I hit 37 homers, drove in 122 runs, and had a .606 slugging percentage as we won 85 games in front of 1.3 million fans. Still, I finished behind Johnny Bench in the NL MVP voting. Bench hit 40 homers and drove in 125 runs in '72. More significantly, his Cincinnati Reds won their division and then the pennant while our Cubs wound up second to the Pirates that year. The Reds would lose the World Series to Oakland in seven games that year. That was the first of three straight championships for Oakland.

Winning the batting crown in 1972 was one of the greatest personal highlights of my big-league career. I was named the Sporting News Player of the Year in '72. While playing in the minors, I always dreamed of winning a big-league batting crown. And a lot of people had told me I was capable of doing that one day. Rogers Hornsby even predicted I would one day win the batting title in the majors.

Realizing at the end of the season that I got a hit once out of every three times I went to the plate was very satisfying. Winning the batting title shows consistency. A lot of things went right for me that summer.

The folks from Louisville Slugger gave me the award for the batting championship. It was a silver bat that I still have. At one time, silver had gone up in price and it was worth quite a bit. But the sentimental value of that award exceeds any amount of money I could have received for it. The award is a reminder to me of the recognition I received that year. When you are talking about winning a batting title in the major leagues, you go around sticking your chest out. It was really incredible to see guys like Tony Gwynn and Rod Carew winning a batting title every year.

Ralph Garr of the Braves was second to me in the chase for the batting title in 1972. He hit .325. Then came Dusty Baker, also of the Braves, at .322, and Cesar Cedeno of Houston at .320.

The fact that we played nothing but day games at Wrigley Field during my era allowed me to keep tabs on Baker and Garr at night. I tried to keep the momentum going throughout the season, and I guess they spurred me on to the title. In later years, Dusty and I would talk about that year and how he and Garr were chasing me.

That year I was actually going for the Triple Crown, but Bench edged me in home runs with 40 and RBIs with 125. I really wanted to win the Triple Crown that year because I figured I needed to win the Triple Crown to win the Most Valuable Player award.

The key to my hitting well in '72 was my patience at the plate. Most of the pitchers I faced were trying so hard not to make a mistake. But I found that if I waited long enough and made them throw me a lot of pitches, at some point I would get a pitch that looked like it was sitting on a tee. I was in such a groove that year. I had tunnel vision and there were times when I focused on nothing but the pitcher's hand. My concentration was so good that it slowed everything down.

My concentration was so good that it slowed everything down.

You used to hear Michael Jordan talking about being in a zone after he would score 50 or 60 points on the basketball court for the Chicago Bulls. Or you would hear Gale Sayers talk about being in a zone when he scored six touchdowns against the San Francisco 49ers at Soldier Field in 1965. I was in a zone in 1972. I got eight hits in a doubleheader against Houston that year—three hits in the first game and five hits in the second game. Every ball I hit was on the nose.

The doubleheader was on July 11, 1972, and I went 8-for-8. I set a league record with 10 straight hits from the previous day. We wound up splitting that doubleheader. Houston won the first game 6–5 with Jimmy Wynn's and Lee May's homers. We won the second game 9–5 when I went 5-for-5 and Rick Monday hit two home runs.

I ended up finishing second again to Johnny Bench for MVP in 1972 and that really bothered me at first. I figured that one of those two years—1970 or '72—I should have won the Most Valuable Player award in the National League. Not taking anything away from my former teammates Kessinger and Beckert, but I didn't have players hitting in front of me to help me collect more RBIs like Bench did in Joe Morgan and Pete Rose. Morgan is a Hall of Famer and Rose is the all-time hits leader.

With the Reds winning the pennant in '72 and people always talking about the "Big Red Machine," that really helped Bench's choice as MVP.

For the most part, I kept my mouth shut during my career, allowing my actions on the field to speak for me. But I felt somewhat disrespected when I did not win the National League Most Valuable Player award in either 1970 or '72. I remember expressing my displeasure and frustration with the following public statement in the Chicago newspapers that year:

"Every year there seems to be a different set of rules. Look at the figures. I was ahead in average and almost even in home runs and RBIs. You have to feel you weren't awarded something you deserved and it's a feeling that sticks with you.

"Well, after 13 years in the big leagues I'm going to let the other guy be the nice guy. I'm going to speak out if I see something. You get tired of people saying it's easy for you to hit .300. It's not easy. It's a lot of work."

I suppose it was my personal misfortune that Bench had two of his best seasons at the same time I was enjoying my best campaigns. When I had my first breakout season in 1970, Bench hit 45 homers and drove in 148 runs at the

Here I am sliding to avoid a tag during my Cubs' playing days.

It felt strange at first when I put on an Oakland A's uniform in 1974 after spending most of my career with the Chicago Cubs. It felt even more awkward to serve as a designated hitter.

I received the Chicago Cubs "Player of the Year" honor in 1972 after winning the National League batting title. Former Chicago sportswriter Jerome Holtzman (center) also presented the Chicago White Sox Player of the Year award to Dick Allen.

Henry Aaron (right) was a smart base runner in addition to being a tremendous slugger. Shown here with Bill Minton, coach of the local semi-pro team, Aaron really wasn't a pull hitter at first. He hit the ball all over the place when I saw him grow up as a cross-handed hitting infielder.

Here I am (on the far left) with Tommie Agee, Amos Otis, and Cleon Jones. At one time the New York Mets had Agee, Jones, and Otis in their outfield. Not bad for a bunch of guys from Alabama. We all went off to play baseball and we wanted to be the best ballplayers up in the big leagues.

Shirley and I enjoyed a Chicago City Hall function with the late Chicago mayor Harold Washington.

It was a pleasure to coach Ryne Sandberg when he first joined the Cubs in the early 1980s. He was a tremendous fielder and exceptional hitter who developed a power stroke. His talent and work ethic made him a Hall of Fame second baseman.

Here are my four girls all grown up. I am a little older than my wife, Shirley. Our teachers would try to keep us separated when we were in school because I was a little older. Well, you see how that worked out. We have four lovely daughters now.

About 30 seconds after receiving the phone call from sportswriter Jack Lang in 1987 that I had been voted into the Hall of Fame, I turned to Shirley and this was my reaction.

Even though I was blessed to be selected for the Hall of Fame in 1987, I often wonder how my baseball legacy might have changed if we had won the World Series in 1969. In the background, Roy Campanella (left) and Ted Williams look on as I deliver my speech.

Willie Mays was born in Westfield, Alabama, just outside of Birmingham.
I felt blessed to join his elite group as a fellow Hall of Famer in 1987. Mays was
the greatest all-around player I ever saw.

Ernie Banks, Ron Santo, Don Kessinger, and I enjoyed some wonderful times together. When I woke up each morning, I couldn't wait to get to the ballpark in 1969. We expected to win every day.

age of 22 to win his first MVP award. Bench, a fellow Hall of Famer, was also known as one of the premier defensive catchers of all time. And, of course, his Reds were winning World Series titles while the Cubs could only knock on the door to the postseason in that era.

Bench was named to 14 All-Star teams in his career and he won 10 straight Gold Gloves.

In 1972 it was Bench who again stood between me and a potential MVP award. In the 1970s with Bench, the Reds appeared in four World Series, winning twice. They reached the postseason six times and wound up second three of the other four seasons.

In the 1972 playoffs, the Reds and the Pittsburgh Pirates went to a deciding fifth game. Trailing 3–2 in the bottom of the ninth in Cincinnati, Bench homered to tie the score and the Reds went on to win the game and the pennant.

My highest salary as a ballplayer was $150,000 in 1973. I remember that after I had the outstanding 1970 season, I wanted $100,000. I wanted to be the first Cubs player to make that much money. But it was a long time before I got it. When spring training started in 1971, I remained home in Chicago for 10 days.

General manager John Holland called me right before spring training was scheduled to start, and I told him I wasn't going to spring training until I signed a contract. I was making $85,000 at the time. Holland said, "I don't know if Mr. Wrigley is going to give you $100,000."

I said, "Well, I will be staying right here in Chicago then."

Finally, after about 10 days, Holland told me that Mr. Wrigley had agreed to pay me $100,000 because of all the things I had done for the ballclub and the organization.

Mr. Wrigley didn't want to pay any ballplayer $100,000. After he relented, he wrote a letter to all of the newspapers in Chicago, telling them what I had done for the team to deserve becoming the first Cub to make $100,000.

I never had an agent as a ballplayer. It wasn't common to have an agent back then. You wanted to keep the good relationship between you and the general manager. I think player agents started becoming more commonplace in 1973 or so. Later in my career with the Cubs I had to go to the office of Mr. Wrigley on Michigan Avenue.

After the 1973 season, the Cubs organization started dismantling the aging nucleus of the ballclub.

I would stroll into the spacious Wrigley Building, right next to the Chicago River. In one of our conversations he said, "Ernie Banks never made $100,000 with the Cubs." I told him, "I'm not Ernie Banks. And Bill Madlock is not going to be like me. We are three different people."

It appeared evident that Mr. Wrigley had a particular problem paying a black man that kind of money. He didn't compare my contract situation with Ron Santo's. He compared me to Ernie Banks.

It seems ludicrous to recall now that we were quibbling over me making $100,000 in 1971. If I were to rack up those kinds of offensive numbers in today's game, I probably could command $15 million a year or more.

But this was a different time in the evolution of the game of baseball. Back then, if you got a $10,000 or $15,000 raise, that was considered great. A lot of guys back then would get only a $2,500 or $3,000 raise. In many instances, for example, a .270 hitter might hit around .270 the next season, so the ballclub would try to pay the guy the same small salary.

Nowadays, of course, it is quite different.

After the 1973 season, the Cubs organization started dismantling the aging nucleus of the ballclub. I survived the first round of purging, but our new manager, Jim Marshall, wanted me to play first base. I did not feel comfortable there, and we ended up losing 96 games that season.

After the 1974 season I was traded to the Oakland A's for Darold Knowles, Bob Locker, and Manny Trillo.

CHAPTER 6

It's Oakland In and Out

It was bittersweet for me to leave the Cubs organization that took a chance on me coming out of high school in Whistler, Alabama, in 1956. But it was probably time for me to move on and join former Cubs teammates Ken Holtzman and Billy North with the A's. And because of the World Series success that Oakland had experienced in the early 1970s with owner Charlie Finley, I figured I had a chance to finally win that elusive World Series ring. What a way to wrap up my career if I could be a part of that!

As a designated hitter, I hit .244 in 1975, with 23 homers and 81 RBIs. I was in a new league and in a different city. I reached a milestone with my 400th career homer on June 12, 1975, in Milwaukee. Hank Aaron also homered that day, so it was a great day for a couple of guys from the area around Mobile, Alabama. It was the eighth homer Aaron had hit for the Brewers and, of course, he went on to finish his amazing career with 755 homers.

When I joined the Oakland A's in 1975, I already knew a lot of guys on the team because Oakland trained in Phoenix all of those years the Cubs were in nearby Mesa, Arizona. Guys like Reggie Jackson, Ken Holtzman, and Billy North were well known to me, and they played their exhibition games at Phoenix Municipal Stadium. Of course, Holtzman and North had been former teammates of mine with the Cubs.

Owner Charlie Finley moved the team from Kansas City to Oakland in the 1968 season. With players such as Rick Monday, Dave Duncan, Sal Bando, Bert Campaneris, Catfish Hunter, Joe Rudi, and Jackson, the Oakland Athletics won five straight American League West titles from 1971–1975. The A's became only the second team (including the Yankees) to win three straight World Series, from 1972–74. We barely failed in 1975 to add a fourth World Series title. We lost to the Red Sox in the playoffs, but at least I was able to play in the postseason for the first time in my 18-year playing career.

And because of the World Series success that Oakland had experienced in the early 1970s with owner Charlie Finley, I figured I had a chance to finally win that elusive World Series ring.

When Reggie was holding out for a new contract from Finley, he would come over to our clubhouse in Mesa during the spring of '70. Reggie would join Ernie Banks and me to play golf after we had played our exhibition games. We would play golf and have some good times together.

Reggie was as confident off the playing field as he was on it. He has always been like that. The same thing was said about Lou Brock as far as being a confident guy. But they could back up what they said with production. That's why Reggie held out for more money from Oakland. He told Finley, "I'm going to hit a lot of home runs for you and I want to be compensated for it."

Finley was a really flamboyant owner who had a lot of ideas and innovations for the game. He even advocated that Major League Baseball use orange baseballs. He lived in Northwest Indiana and had played semi-pro baseball before making a lot of money in the life insurance business.

He used to trot out a mule named "Charley O" around the field and even into hotel lobbies. He introduced ballgirls and a mechanical rabbit that gave new baseballs to the umpire. Finley also recommended playing World Series games at night to maximize fan interest. That was one idea that really caught on and made Major League Baseball an awful lot of money over the years.

Reggie Jackson had hit 47 homers in 1969. When Reggie held out for more money, Finley threatened to send him back to the minors. Vida Blue, a Cy Young Award-winning pitcher, also had a prolonged contract dispute with Finley in 1971. It took the commissioner, Bowie Kuhn, to settle that dispute.

Finley also tried to exercise his power in the 1973 World Series. Oakland infielder Mike Andrews made two straight errors in the twelfth inning of a loss to the Mets. Dick Williams, the A's manager then, and several teammates came to Andrew's defense in the matter. After Oakland won the World Series that year, Williams resigned and Finley named Alvin Dark the new manager.

Oakland won another World Series title in 1974, but Catfish Hunter was declared a free agent by an arbitrator because Finley had failed to make contractually stipulated payments for Hunter into an insurance annuity fund. Even without Hunter, we easily won the division in 1975. In the spring of 1976, Finley traded Jackson to the Baltimore Orioles.

While Reggie was holding out in 1970 I think he missed the game of baseball quite a bit. But Ernie and I really tried to support him during his holdout.

When I joined the A's in 1975, Jackson was starting to enter that category of superstardom.

I recall Reggie had to go to the doctor one day because he had hives. The doctor told him that he had to start letting his emotions out instead of keeping them bottled up. That's all Reggie needed to hear. Most people have always seen Reggie Jackson being an outgoing, extroverted individual.

On a trip to Anaheim to play the Angels one time, Reggie realized that his favorite bat was not in the rack. He had been something like 15-for-20 with eight or nine home runs with that favorite bat. But he had left that bat in Oakland and the equipment man had forgotten to put it in the bat bag. We were getting ready to take batting practice in Anaheim and Reggie was running around the clubhouse yelling, "Where's my bat?" But nobody could find that particular bat, so Reggie took batting practice with another bat.

Finally, it was time for the game to get started against the Angels. I was batting fifth as the designated hitter and Reggie was the cleanup hitter. Up until the last minute, Reggie thought someone would find his special bat, but it did not happen. The Angels pitcher delivered a fastball right down the middle of the plate, and Reggie popped it straight up in the air. He was really pissed.

Down in the visitors' dugout in Anaheim, they used to line up the bats in the bat rack in the little entryway to the clubhouse. Reggie returned to the dugout after popping up and he took one of those weighted lead bats that hitters use in the on-deck circle. He had fire in his eyes, and he took that lead bat and started breaking every bat in the rack that was lined up there. He started yelling, "Get my damn bat here!"

That next night that we played, as you might imagine, Reggie's favorite bat was right there with him in Anaheim.

Reggie had a more compassionate side to him as well. I remember that Jimmy Bank, now the Cubs' traveling secretary, was the Oakland A's traveling secretary back in the 1970s. Reggie proposed an idea for us to have adjoining hotel rooms on the road, with another room in the middle where the two of us could meet to talk baseball if we wanted to. He said if we didn't feel like going to that middle room to talk baseball, or if we wanted our privacy, it would be no big deal and we would just shut the door. Reggie said that it was an idea he had because he respected me as a top player with the Cubs and appreciated my veteran expertise. I thought that was very nice of him.

When I joined the Oakland A's in 1975, I already knew a lot of guys on the team because Oakland trained in Phoenix all of those years the Cubs were in nearby Mesa, Arizona.

Reggie would say, "I can't relate to these other guys on this team, I need to relate to a superstar." That's the way Reggie would talk. So he went to Jimmy Bank with that proposal and it worked out great that summer. We would always tell other people that we were cousins and such, just having fun with them.

In his home in California Reggie had all sorts of fancy cars that he used to dicker with, and he still does. He has always done everything first class and with a flair.

A couple of years ago, Reggie had a golf tournament at Pebble Beach. He asked if I wanted to come there to play. I told him I would come if I could get a good flight out there. He said: "I will get you a good flight."

Reggie sent a private plane to pick Shirley and me up! We went to the airport in Waukegan, Illinois, to board that plane and then we flew it to Pebble Beach, California. Frank Robinson was also on the plane. And we picked up Sal Bando along the way in Phoenix. We stayed out there for three days and we went out and played golf. Then the plane brought us back to Waukegan. It was a tremendous convenience, a different world.

Reggie was as confident off the playing field as he was on it.

Reggie was a good-hearted guy, but his temper would flare up if anybody crossed him. Reggie and Billy North got into a fight in the clubhouse one time over in Detroit.

North was in Reggie's locker when Reggie approached him. I am not sure what actually precipitated the fight, but he wrestled Billy into the locker. They were like two big bulls in that little, cramped locker room in the old Tiger Stadium. They wrestled and struggled for about 30 minutes. Then after it seemed to simmer down, they sat in front of their lockers and started staring at each other again. Then they went at it again. Ray Fosse, the A's catcher, tried to step in and stop them. That's how he re-injured his shoulder. Fosse initially injured his shoulder when Pete Rose crashed into him at home plate in the 1970 All-Star Game.

Jackson and North didn't speak to each other for a long time. It's too bad, because Billy North was a lovable guy who never bothered anybody. He was a real smart guy who used to sit on the plane and work crossword puzzles. I think his mother was a schoolteacher. He was a great center fielder and a daring base runner.

Alvin Dark was the Oakland manager in 1975, and I found him to be a pretty good guy despite some allegations of him being a racist in earlier years. Maybe he had changed by the time I got there. He was a Christian man. Then, in 1976, Chuck Tanner became the A's manager.

We were flying from Boston to Oakland one time and North noticed that the players in the front of the plane were getting better food than the players in the back, where he was sitting. Everyone on the team should have been getting the same food. Bando was the players' representative for Oakland, so North went to complain to Bando. He said, "What the heck is going on? We should be getting the same food as the other guys."

Apparently, it was just a case where the airline didn't have enough food onboard so that everybody could receive the same food. Chuck Tanner heard the commotion and complaining and he walked to the back of the plane. I looked toward the back of the plane and I noticed Tanner pointing his finger and pushing North in the chest, telling North to keep quiet and stop complaining. I could see Billy getting mad.

So I got up out of my seat and I went back there to calm things down. I knew that Billy had a short fuse and he was about to explode. It could have been a very ugly situation. When Tanner returned to the front of the plane, I went over to him and told him, "Chuck, you owe Billy an apology because he is only doing the right thing. He should have the same meal as everybody else is having."

Tanner said, "You think that's right, Billy?"

I said, "Yeah, that's right. Go back there and apologize to Billy, because we are going to need this guy the rest of the season. If we want to win the division and if we want to go to the World Series, we are going to have to have this guy."

I was able to reason with Chuck because he and I had played together with the Cubs.

The one thing that always will stick with me about those Oakland teams was how they reacted to wins and losses.

At that point, Chuck went back there to talk to North again, and he apologized. That simmered things down and the two of them seemed to have a good relationship the rest of the year. The two of them forgot about the argument and Billy went on to have an outstanding season.

When I was with Oakland, there was something happening in the clubhouse every evening. We had Willie McCovey and Nate Colbert with the A's in 1976 too. All we did was DH, and that is what Finley wanted us to do. I had told Finley that I could still play in the field. But he said, "I have players who can play in the field and catch the ball. All I want you to do is come up and hit four times a game. You can go ahead and eat a hot dog during the game and do anything you want. But just be ready to hit."

I had so much fun those two years. I was living out in Walnut Creek, California. Ray Fosse and a couple of other guys used to ride back and forth from the ballpark with me. When I first came to the Oakland ballclub as a coach in 1983, the owner gave us all credit cards and automobiles to ride around in all of the time.

One of our biggest fans in Oakland was a young kid named Stanley Burrell. Finley saw this kid outside the stadium one day and saw him singing and performing. Finley was impressed with him and told him was going to make him an honorary executive vice president.

Burrell used to hang out around the clubhouse all of the time, sometimes serving as our batboy. Meanwhile, Finley would be back in Chicago, and his secretary in Oakland, Carol, would make sure Finley could listen to our games. All of us players were certain that Burrell was a snoop or informer for Finley, to let him know what we were all up to. Rollie Fingers was one of the guys who never trusted Burrell in the clubhouse.

"Get out of here! We're having a private conversation," Fingers would say to the kid. Or, "Everybody keep quiet. Here comes Pipeline." That's what we called Burrell.

I still have some pictures of us all celebrating in the clubhouse after winning the division title in 1975. Burrell, at the age of 12 or 13, was in the clubhouse with us as we celebrating with champagne.

Years later, I am walking through my house and I see this guy performing on television. He is singing and jumping all around. Shirley said, "You know him. It's MC Hammer. He used to be the batboy in Oakland."

Hammer once came to Chicago and I got him tickets to go to a Cubs game. But something came up at the last minute and he couldn't make it to the ballpark. He was a real nice kid and we had a lot of fun with him.

The one thing that always will stick with me about those Oakland teams was how they reacted to wins and losses. If we lost a tough game, the guys would drink a beer, sit around for a little bit, then they were gone. If we won a big game by scoring three or four runs in the last inning, we would come in and drink a beer, talk a little about the game, and then were gone.

I interpreted that as a matter of learning how to handle losing before you can learn how to win. You don't accept losing, but you don't dwell on the game that you lost. We didn't get too high when we won a baseball game. We had the confidence that we would win the next one. They were a great bunch of guys who knew how to play the game. And it seemed like every time we got in a position to close out a game, Rollie Fingers was there.

> **I knew that the American League was a breaking ball league. In the National League, it was more aggressive.**

At the end of the season, if we needed a big run or a big hit, Bando was there. If we needed a great defensive play, Campaneris was there. If we needed a stolen base, Billy North was there. If we needed a home run, Gene Tenace was there. If we needed a big catch, Joe Rudi was there.

When Billy North was ready to break Campaneris's franchise stolen-base record, Campaneris would swing and foul every time Billy would take off to steal. It got to be a running joke that everybody had a good laugh about.

When Finley tried to sell Fingers and Rudi to Boston in 1976, the commissioner, Bowie Kuhn, didn't let it go through.

Then Finley tried to deal Blue to the Yankees, but the only way the deal could go through was if Blue already had a signed contract with Oakland. So Finley called Blue into his office and said, "Come on in, Vida. We're going to sign you to a new contract."

As soon as Vida signed that contract, he was traded to the Yankees and Vida was mad.

Finley insisted he needed the money to sign free agents and rebuild. Kuhn voided the sales of Rudi, Fingers, and Blue as not being "in the best interests of baseball." Kuhn later voided another sale of Blue, to the Cincinnati Reds. Meanwhile, major league players won the right to play out their options, and seven A's did so in 1976.

As a team, we protested the sale of those guys to Boston and we refused to take the field. We all said that we would forfeit the rest of the season if we had to. Our player rep, Jim Todd, remained in communication with Finley and kept telling him that we were determined as a team not to take the field without those guys.

About 20 minutes before the game was scheduled to start, Todd made a last-ditch call to Finley and emphasized that the team was not going to take the field without those other guys. Finally, about 10 minutes before the scheduled start of the game, Finley called Todd back and told him that Rudi and Fingers were reinstated. He said, "Joe Rudi is going to play left field today. Rollie Fingers, if you need him, is going to pitch. You guys got me this time."

When we all walked out of the clubhouse and took the field and Rudi took left field, the crowd of about 20,000 or 30,000 gave us a standing ovation. It was a real rarity in baseball. Kansas City beat us that year in the division race, but we took an important stand as players.

One other important thing I noticed about the A's as a team was their closeness off the field. During that era,

CB radios were all the rage and we each had one. Each player had a unique handle. I was "The Whistler," Kenny Holtzman was "Ball4," Gene Tenace was "Steamboat," and Joe Rudi was "Highball." When the games were over, we would be talking to each other on the CBs until we got home. It was a fun two years for me out there.

After the 1976 season, I was ready to retire from base-ball. In 1975, of course, I was a designated hitter for the first time in my career. But we won a division for the first time in my career and we were playing good baseball. We were playing good baseball in September and it was a great feeling. I drove in 84 runs and hit 23 home runs in 1975 with a new franchise. I just had to get used to being a designated hitter because in previous years I was able to relax when I took my position in left field.

> I believe my quiet, unassuming ways played a part in my having a lower profile than Ernie.

It took me a while to get used to the different style of pitching in the American League. I had talked to Jackson in Arizona about American League pitching before I joined the A's. I knew that the American League was a breaking ball league. In the National League, it was more aggressive. With a 2-ball, 1-strike count, you would probably get a hard slider or something fast. In the American League, you might get a change-up or a slow curveball.

I noticed the change in pitching style by watching Holtzman, who changed his tactics in the American League after doing things differently with the Cubs. Reggie told me that I had to be a free-swinger in the American League, ready to hit. You just have to see the ball and hit it. Don't sit on a certain pitch and expect to see it.

When Aaron came over to the American League with the Brewers he said, "I've had enough of this mess." You can't guess with them because they throw a lot of slow stuff. The Brewers have since switched to the National League.

Bobby Bonds said the same thing when he played in the American League late in his career.

My first summer away from playing baseball in 1977 was an interesting experience. I was so used to the routine of going to the ballpark and to spring training. But I was in Loomis, California, having a new home built. I had purchased 25 acres about 17 miles north of Sacramento. That kept me really busy and I think that helped in my transition from the playing field. I had a lake out there on the property that allowed me to go fishing. During that first year away from baseball, I couldn't sit there and watch an entire game on television. I would watch an inning or two, then I would get up and walk out of the room to do something else. It is just tough for any baseball player to break away from the game that had been your way of life for so many years.

But now, suddenly, I was able to spend a lot of time at home and with my kids. It was very enjoyable, along with the house being built. Also, my brother, Franklin, was living in Sacramento, so we were able to spend a lot of time together. He and I would go to Lake Tahoe and Reno for fun times. We would tell our wives that we would be back at about midnight. It was just fun times.

I came back to Chicago in 1980 as a coach. Bob Kennedy, the Cubs general manager, had called me in 1979 and asked me to go to the minor leagues and work with the hitters. I worked with a guy named C.B. Davis, who was a good baseball man, and we had a lot of fun together. Kennedy guaranteed me a job in the major leagues in two years after working with the minor leaguers. This was when Joe Carter, Mel Hall, and several other good Cubs prospects were in the minors. I worked with Cubs minor league teams in Midland, Texas, and Geneva, New York. I would go out to work with these players for about 10 days, then I would go back home to California.

I was gardening and fishing and doing things with the kids at home. It was a relaxing time in my life. After the two years I got the job with the big-league club in Chicago, just as Kennedy had promised. That's when Shirley and I decided to sell our house in California and move back to the Chicago area. Before I was traded to Oakland, we lived in Glen Ellyn, Illinois, for 14 months. I found it to be a great community, so we decided to move back to Glen Ellyn. And that's where we are now.

As I look back at my career I have mostly fond memories of playing in Chicago and Oakland. We had three Hall of Famers on those Cubs teams: Ernie Banks, Fergie Jenkins, and me. And in my mind, Ron Santo was a Hall of Famer as well. Ernie, of course, is known as "Mr. Cub," and sometimes people ask me if I resent that I am sometimes overlooked.

From time to time, it might have bothered me a little because Ernie was hitting home runs and I was hitting home runs. He was putting people in the seats and I was putting people in the seats. But I knew that Ernie had been in Chicago a long time, way before I had joined the club. When I got here, Ernie was The Man. And he has the rightful name of "Mr. Cub." I just couldn't figure out why in the hell he could hit so many home runs. He was the only one who could hit the ball out of the ballpark consistently on the Cubs before I came here. It baffles me why pitchers didn't pitch around Ernie.

I believe my quiet, unassuming ways played a part in my having a lower profile than Ernie.

I always was a believer that you can't talk and listen. I observed things and I listened. Reporters would come in the locker room and ask me questions. I would give them direct answers. I didn't give them a lot of propaganda; I just told them what they wanted to know. Maybe I should have broadened my answers. But that's the way I was as an individual.

When I first came to the big leagues, I would overhear Ernie when the writers would interview him and he was very popular with the media. I also noticed that Santo would expound upon answers to the questions they asked him. But I was more direct in my approach and that is the way I have always been. I didn't get too high when I went 4-for-4 and I didn't get too low when I went 0-for-4.

I didn't take the game home with me, either. I didn't even pay a whole lot of attention to who the pitcher for the opposing team was going to be the next day. I didn't want to fog my mind overnight. I wanted to come out to the ballpark, do what I had to do, and start playing the game.

CHAPTER 7

The Right Necessities

In 1987, several years after I had left the Oakland A's as a player, I began to coach for the Cubs when Dallas Green was the general manager. I remember in September of that year being involved in a meeting with Dallas and all of the other Cubs coaches when we were ready to start the fall Instructional League in Arizona. Dallas asked me if I wanted to go out and run the Cubs' entry in the Instructional League. It took me about two weeks to think it over. I really wanted to manage in the major leagues at the time because I thought I had enough experience to do it. After being in the major leagues for so long and being around longtime baseball mentors such as Leo Durocher and Bob Kennedy...I knew that I could do it.

The Cubs had a managing vacancy at the time after Jim Frey had been fired in the middle of the 1986 season and Gene Michael was hired as the interim manager to finish out the season.

It is understood that being a big-league manager is a volatile job. Frey had been voted National League Manager of the Year in 1984 after surprisingly leading the Cubs to the NL East championship and to within a couple of innings of the Cubs' first appearance in a World Series in 39 years.

The 1984 Cubs defied all odds. They were a team that had finished fifth the previous season with a 71–91 mark. The Cubs had lost 11 straight exhibition games in the spring of '84 and finished with the worst exhibition record in all of baseball. Then they suddenly ruled their division with a 96–65 record—a turnaround of 25 games.

"I've got a plan," Frey announced confidently that spring training during the 11-game losing streak. Frey, known as "Preacher Man" behind his back by the players, didn't know then how prophetic his statement would be.

When a team performs poorly for an extended period of time, the manager usually pays the price.

The '84 Cubs had a lot to overcome, including each other. During spring training in 1984, a strange intra-squad fight took place before a game against the San Diego Padres in Yuma, Arizona.

During batting practice that hot, sultry afternoon, Cubs pitcher Dick Ruthven was picking up baseballs near second base and dutifully placing them in a basket. When Ruthven saw cocky young Mel Hall stroll by without offering to help, the veteran asked, "You think you're too good to pick up the baseballs?"

With that, Hall decked Ruthven and the two continued slugging it out. Other Cubs quickly jumped in behind second base as dust rose from the infield at Desert Sun Stadium.

Frey immediately sent Hall to the right-field bullpen to cool off. Ruthven was sent to another area on the field. Meanwhile, Frey gathered the rest of his team in center field for an impromptu lecture.

"I don't want selfish, individualistic attitudes on this team," Frey said. "Anyone who can't go along with the program can go play with somebody else."

Hall was traded to Cleveland on June 13 with Joe Carter in the deal that brought Rick Sutcliffe to the Cubs.

Rookie Cubs pitchers Reggie Patterson and Bill Johnson also got into a fight in the spring of 1984. Patterson gained notoriety in 1985 for giving up hit number 4,191 to Pete Rose, which tied him with Ty Cobb for the all-time lead.

Ryne Sandberg, then 24, was the NL Most Valuable Player in 1984, hitting .314 with a league-high 114 runs scored, 36 doubles, 19 homers, and a .520 slugging percentage. It was the signature season of his great career.

At the conclusion of that regular season the Cubs faced the West Division champion San Diego Padres in a best-of-five League Championship Series, won by the Padres after the Cubs had taken a 2–0 lead at Wrigley Field. Needing to win just once in San Diego, they dropped all three. The Cubs had a 3–0 lead with Rick Sutcliffe on the mound when the Padres rallied to win 6–3 in Game 5.

First baseman Leon Durham, who had a .994 career fielding percentage, watched a hard-hit ground ball go through his legs in the seventh inning, and that opened up the floodgates for a Padres comeback. Durham acknowledges that one of his teammates accidentally knocked over a bucket of Gatorade on his first baseman's mitt in the dugout before he committed that fateful error in the '84 playoffs.

Cubs fans were disappointed about losing in such dramatic fashion, of course. But 1984 was mostly a fun season for the fans, just as 1969 was before we shed our division lead to the New York Mets. Expectations were high for the 1985 season and ticket sales at Wrigley Field had hit record levels.

But numerous injuries had decimated the Cubs' roster in 1985, and 1986 started out poorly for the team as well. When a team performs poorly for an extended period of time, the manager usually pays the price.

Catcher Jody Davis was afflicted with an intestinal virus in 1985, forcing him to miss a crucial part of the season when the Cubs lost 13 games in a row. The Cubs fell from first place in early June to fourth place and 23-and-one-half games out of first by the end of the season. The entire Cubs starting pitching staff spent time on the disabled list in 1985, as well as center fielder Bobby Dernier and several other key performers.

The four original starting pitchers—Sutcliffe, Dennis Eckersley, Steve Trout, and Scott Sanderson—missed a total of 52 starts. All four were on the disabled list in August. Ruthven, the fifth starter, missed nine starts. The Cubs lost another 242 games from position players because of injuries.

The disappointment of the 1985 season was felt throughout the city of Chicago as the Cubs nonetheless drew a record attendance that year. They set a city and franchise attendance record by drawing 2,161,534 paid fans to Wrigley Field. They also led the National League in road attendance by attracting a club-record 2,255,306 fans.

After contemplating the offer from Green, I finally decided I would go to the Instructional League in 1987. As it turned out, I went out there and I had so much fun. It was a terrific experience and a great way to wind up a whirlwind year that saw me inducted into the Baseball Hall of Fame that summer.

Joe Girardi was out there playing, and Jerome Walton, Derrick May, and Heathcliff Slocumb...all of the top prospects in the organization. I used to get in the batting cage and hit. I was really active at that time—I was 49 years old—and I could show them how to run the bases and such.

Dallas Green, of course, had come over to the Cubs from the Philadelphia organization in 1981. One of his friends from Philadelphia watched me manage some games in the Instructional League that fall and said, "After watching you make all of the right moves and the strategy you used in Arizona, you could manage in the big leagues right now." That was something I already knew. I didn't have to have anybody tell me that. But it made me feel reassured to hear it from someone else who knows a lot about the game of baseball.

After contemplating the offer from Green, I finally decided I would go to the Instructional League in 1987. As it turned out, I went out there and I had so much fun.

One of the most important things I attempted to do in the Instructional League that year was to convert about five guys into switch-hitters. During the 1980s, I had seen how Whitey Herzog's St. Louis Cardinals were so dangerous offensively because they had five or six switch-hitters in their lineup. That gave Herzog so much flexibility as a manager, especially in the late innings when the opposing team brought in relief pitchers. Switch-hittters like Ozzie Smith, Tommie Herr, Terry Pendleton, Vince Coleman, and Willie McGee gave opposing pitchers and managers fits. Especially when the Cardinals played on their home AstroTurf at Busch Stadium. They were able to manufacture so many runs with their speed and aggressiveness. They would bunt for base hits, use the hit-and-run, and beat out slow ground balls or high bouncers in the infield for base hits.

I used to work with guys like Walton to try to get them to become switch-hitters. Batting only right-handed in the big leagues, he would later become the National League Rookie of the Year in 1989 when he hit .293 with 24 stolen bases. But when I left the Instructional League, I guess the new coaches stopped teaching those guys how to become switch-hitters. We could have had so many more good young ballplayers if they could have done that.

The Cubs had never had a black manager in their franchise history up until the 1980s.

At the end of the six weeks in the Instructional League in 1987, Dallas Green came out to Arizona to meet with me. I asked him then to let me come to Chicago to become the new manager of the Cubs. I assured him about the things I know about the game. Dallas said, "No, we're going to get somebody with experience."

He said, "You know what, Billy, I would like you to go and manage in Triple A at Iowa."

At the time, I wasn't ready to go manage at Triple A. I said, "I have to go talk to Shirley. I don't know about this."

The entire proposition seemed unsettling to me. I felt as if they were just trying to get me out of Chicago and I didn't want to do that. They had given me no promises or assurances for my future in baseball at that point. They simply said, "You go manage Triple A and we will see what happens after that."

Gordon Goldsberry, who was in charge of the Cubs' minor league system then, kept calling me to find out my decision. I kept asking for a little more time. I had a trip to New York scheduled to be on a television show that Tim McCarver hosted. On the way back home I said to myself, "I can't take the managing job in Triple A. I have too much experience in the big leagues." So I was prepared to tell Dallas that I couldn't do it.

If I had been assured that I would get the Cubs managing position after managing at Triple A, I would have done it at the drop of a hat. But there were no such assurances.

America's pastime truly had not been all-American in terms of fair hiring practices.

I was supposed to have a meeting with Dallas in Chicago later that morning after returning from New York. As I came into the house that morning, a friend of mine called. He said, "Dallas just got fired and somebody else is taking over the ballclub." I was shocked.

Green, now 73, has spent 52 years in baseball as a pitcher, manager, general manager, president, and now senior advisor to Phillies general manager Pat Gillick.

If the Cubs had won—or even made it to—the World Series in 1984, Green might still be the team's president/general manager.

Known for his abrupt and candid nature, Green managed the Phillies to their first World Series title in 1980. After being hired by the Tribune Company as GM in 1981, he imported several coaches and scouts from the Phillies. Lee Elia, who was Green's college roommate at the University of Delaware, became his first Cubs manager.

Of course Elia became the prime example of how a major league manager could become stressed out. In 1983, Elia delivered a profanity-laced press conference after a home loss to the Pirates.

Here is a sanitized transcript of the tirade:

> [Bleep] those [bleep]in' fans who come out here and say they're Cub fans that are supposed to be behind you, rippin' every [bleep]ing thing you do. I'll tell you one [bleep]ing thing, I hope we get [bleep]ing hotter than [bleep], just to stuff it up them 3,000 [bleep]ing people that show up every [bleep]ing day, because if they're the real Chicago [bleep]ing fans, they can kiss my [bleep]ing ass right downtown, and print it!
>
> They're really, really behind you around here... my [bleep]ing ass. What the [bleep] am I supposed to do, go out there and let my [bleep]ing players get destroyed every day and be quiet about it? For the [bleep]ing nickel-dime people who turn up? The [bleep]ers don't even work. That's why they're out at the [bleep]ing game. They oughta go out and get a [bleep]ing job and find out what it's like to go out and earn a [bleep]ing living. Eighty-five percent of the [bleep]ing world is working. The other fifteen percent come out here. A [bleep]ing playground for the [bleep]ers. Rip them [bleep]ers. Rip them [bleep]ing [bleep]ers like the [bleep]ing players. We got guys bustin' their [bleep]ing ass, and

them [bleep]ing people boo. And that's the Cubs? My players get around here. I haven't seen it this [bleep]ing year. Everybody associated with this organization have been winners their whole [bleeping] life. Everybody. And the credit is not given in that respect.

All right, they don't show because we're 5 and 14... and unfortunately, that's the criteria of them dumb 15 [bleep]ing percent that come out to day baseball. The other 85 percent are earning a living. I tell you, it'll take more than a 5 and 12 or 5 and 14 to destroy the makeup of this club. I guarantee you that. There's some [bleep]ing pros out there that wanna win. But you're stuck in a [bleep]ing stigma of the [bleep]ing Dodgers and the Phillies and the Cardinals and all that cheap [bleep]. It's unbelievable. It really is. It's a disheartening [bleep]ing situation that we're in right now. Anybody who was associated with the Cub organization four or five years ago that came back and sees the multitude of progress that's been made will understand that if they're baseball people, that 5 and 14 doesn't negate all that work. We got 143 [bleep]ing games left.

What I'm tryin' to say is don't rip them [bleep]ing guys out there. Rip me. If you wanna rip somebody, rip my [bleep]ing ass. But don't rip them [bleep]ing guys 'cause they're givin' everything they can give. And right now they're tryin' to do more than God gave 'em, and that's why we make the simple mistakes. That's exactly why.

Also, in the early 1980s, John Vukovich came from the Phillies as a coach and Gordon Goldsberry was brought in as the team's director of player development. It is hard for me realize that both Vukovich and Goldsberry have passed on. Then Green went to work making numerous key trades with the Phillies, acquiring Keith Moreland, Dan Larson, and Dickie Noles.

In the long run, that racist statement that Campanis made was good for black people, in a roundabout way, because it made people aware of the prejudices that still exist and it made Major League Baseball finally take some positive action to rectify the problem.

The blockbuster deal came during that first off-season when Green sent Ivan DeJesus to the Phillies for shortstop Larry Bowa and minor league infielder Ryne Sandberg. Bowa was the Cubs' starting shortstop for three seasons and, of course, Sandberg who was considered a throw-in on the deal at the time, was inducted into the Hall of Fame in 2005.

Green continued to usurp Phillies talent when he acquired left fielder Gary Matthews and center fielder Bob Dernier before the 1984 season. During that division championship season, Green also picked up pitcher Dennis Eckersley from the Red Sox in exchange for first baseman Bill Buckner in late May. Then he sent outfielders Mel Hall and Joe Carter to the Indians for relief pitcher George Frazier, backup catcher Ron Hassey, and right-handed pitcher

Rick Sutcliffe in mid-June. Sutcliffe went 16–1 with the Cubs that season and won the Cy Young Award.

I wound up staying in Chicago as a big-league coach. But who knows, maybe if I had gone to manage at Triple A I would have been the manager of the Cubs later. It is all speculation at this point.

The Cubs had never had a black manager in their franchise history up until the 1980s. It could have been a factor in their reluctance to give me a chance at that point. Of course, in the 1990s Don Baylor became the Cubs' first-ever black manager, followed by Dusty Baker. The Cubs had gone more than a century without an African American manager and then suddenly hired two in a row. Baker had previously guided the San Francisco Giants to the World Series, losing to the Anaheim Angels in seven games.

You get some jobs because you can hit the ball out of the ballpark and you are a big fan favorite of the Chicago Cubs. But there are other jobs in baseball that you don't get unless the person hiring is comfortable with you.

In 1997, in connection with the 40th anniversary of Jackie Robinson breaking the color barrier in Major League Baseball, the ABC *Nightline* program interviewed former Los Angeles Dodgers general manager Al Campanis, who helped assemble teams that won four National League pennants and the 1981 World Series champions.

The show's then-host, Ted Koppel, asked Campanis why there were so few black managers in baseball at the time, and no black general managers. Campanis, who had played alongside Robinson and had signed several top minority players as a GM, shocked viewers of the show by saying that blacks lacked "the necessities" to be managers and executives. Campanis went on to make other racist comments about blacks, including stating that blacks are often poor swimmers "because they lack buoyancy."

Koppel repeatedly tried to allow Campanis to remove his foot from his mouth by saying, "Do you really believe that?" But Campanis would not immediately recant. He was pressured to resign from his position two days after the comments. He tried to clarify his comments the next year, but the damage had been done. He died on June 21, 1998, of coronary artery disease.

The 2007 Chicago Cubs have five or six African American players, and I think we must be among the leaders in the league in that category.

I think that when Don Baylor, Dusty Baker, and Cito Gaston were able to take over ballclubs as managers, organizations found out that these guys had played the game and they knew how to run a baseball team as well as any other manager. It's just a matter of getting the respect of the players. Dusty and Cito have shown that they can take a team to the World Series.

When Baylor got fired, I had a meeting with Andy MacPhail, who was the Cubs president at the time, and then general manager Ed Lynch. I had been the bench coach and I had been the first-base coach. So I again inquired about the managing job. I had an interview with MacPhail and Lynch. I don't know if that was just window dressing or what. I hope not. I came in and I made good spiel about what I would do with the ballclub. But somebody else got the job.

When historic events happen during your lifetime, immediately you remember where you were at that time. Like when Martin Luther King was assassinated in 1968. We were playing an exhibition game in Lafayette, Indiana. When President Kennedy was shot in 1963, I was driving down Davis Avenue in Mobile, Alabama.

And when Al Campanis made the statement on national television that "blacks don't have the necessities" to become major league managers or general managers, I was sitting on the end of our bed watching the interview. I turned to Shirley and said, "What is this guy saying? You can't say that kind of stuff. There have been so many smart guys who know the game who happen to be black. Guys like Maury Wills and so many others."

The other disturbing aspect of his comments was the fact that Campanis had been around Jackie Robinson and he could see what a smart player he was, a college-educated man with tremendous baseball savvy and intellect.

By the time the firestorm surrounding his racist comments made the rounds, Major League Baseball was forced to respond by providing more opportunities for minorities in management and front-office positions. It encouraged Dusty Baker, for instance, to pursue a position as a manager with the San Francisco Giants.

America's pastime truly had not been all-American in terms of fair hiring practices. The color barrier for players was not broken until Jackie Robinson was given an opportunity with the Brooklyn Dodgers more than a half century ago. Frank Robinson became the first African American manager in the big leagues in 1975 with the Cleveland Indians.

Baseball commissioner Bud Selig is acutely aware of the inequities that have existed when it comes to hiring minorities for positions of authority in baseball.

MacPhail, now the president of the Baltimore Orioles, was quoted in the *Chicago Tribune* as saying, "It has long been an initiative of the commissioner to try to ensure that a wide spectrum of people at least get the opportunity to be considered for major league managing jobs, major league coaching jobs. To the extent that he implemented a process where any club that goes through a managerial change has to report back to Major League Baseball how many they interviewed and who they interviewed.

Somebody has to tell them to be patient and believe in themselves, because great things could be there on the horizon if they hang in there.

"That also helps other clubs that might be looking for changes. It gives them an idea or a road map as to whom they might hire. Teams are motivated solely by who they think might give them the best chance to win as many games as they possibly can.

"I think the strategy that has been laid out has been an effective one," MacPhail continued. "Making the clubs aware of the best candidates. Then what happens, happens. There are minority managers now that are hired and fired, which is the normal course of events in sports. Baseball is no different. And I think the commissioner should be proud that our sport has as representative a percentage of diverse managers. Not just African Americans, but Hispanics and whatever. In the final analysis, clubs are under so much scrutiny and pressure. They just are going to do what they think is going to help them win the most games. That should be the bottom line and I believe that is the bottom line."

I respected Dusty Baker when he was the manager of the Cubs, but so many of his critics talked about him not knowing the Xs and Os of the game. I didn't like that because he is a smart manager. When Dusty first got the job with the Cubs, there were so many free agents saying they now wanted to come to Chicago because of Dusty. White players, black players, and Hispanics all wanted to play for Dusty. They respected him as a manager and as a man. That's half the battle. Then guys have to go out and play hard for you.

In the long run, that racist statement that Campanis made was good for black people, in a roundabout way, because it made people aware of the prejudices that still exist and it made Major League Baseball finally take some positive action to rectify the problem. A lot of minorities got jobs, and everyone could see that minorities could manage a ballclub and take it all the way to the top.

I have tried my best not to become bitter about failing to have an opportunity to manage in the big leagues. The whole experience just helped me realize that politics play an important role in getting a managing position. You have to have people who believe in you and who are comfortable around you. Certain general managers are pretty comfortable around their guys. For instance, when Ed Lynch was the Cubs general manager, he brought in Jim Riggleman to manage the Cubs. That was at least in part because the two of them had been together in San Diego with the Padres organization. Riggleman knew the game really well, and I think he could be a good manager if he gets a chance again. I just wish I could have had that one chance.

I am not bitter at all. You get some jobs because you can hit the ball out of the ballpark and you are a big fan favorite of the Chicago Cubs. But there are other jobs in baseball that you don't get unless the person hiring is comfortable with you.

> **Baseball is a game of failure. If you don't get a hit two out of three times, you are hitting .300 and doing a great job.**

In the last several years we are getting minorities in the right positions of power to make the decisions to hire and fire individuals in the game of baseball. The Chicago White Sox, for instance, have Ken Williams as the general manager, and he guided them to a World Series title in 2005. And his manager was Ozzie Guillen, a Hispanic.

Players from my era, even Hall of Famers like Ernie Banks, Hank Aaron, and I, didn't make the kind of money to eventually become owners of a ballclub. It is my hope that minority players today who are making $10, $15, and $20 million a year will be able to pull together and own a big-league ballclub one day. Eventually I think these players' agents will convince them to do that. The players are part of this industry and they can dictate how we are going to play this game in the future.

There have been many theories advanced as to why there is a dwindling number of African American ballplayers in the big leagues. The 2007 Chicago Cubs have five or six African American players, and I think we must be among the leaders in the league in that category. I think the great success and popularity of Michael Jordan with the Chicago Bulls influenced a lot of young black kids to pursue an NBA career instead of a baseball career. I also feel the popularity of the National Football League has attracted so many big and strong young African American athletes.

Many of the colleges and universities in the South that denied admission to blacks when I was growing up are now recruiting and offering four-year scholarships in both basketball and football to young men who could also excel in baseball or sign right out of high school to play professional baseball. That's what happened to me.

But it is a slower process to make it to the big leagues in baseball. You have to go to the minor leagues first and everything is a lot less glamorous. In basketball, if you are 19 or 20 years old and you can play the game, people figure you can step right into the NBA and make millions of dollars. And in the NFL, after your college career, you can sign a big contract and then make a major impact in the league in a year or two.

When you look at the bigger picture with baseball, you can have greater longevity than football and maybe basketball. But you can get to the so-called Promised Land of basketball and football a little quicker.

The other attractive aspect of basketball for the inner-city kids is that it costs very little to get a basketball and find a few buddies to have a game. Baseball requires 18 players, a baseball field, and more expensive equipment to play a game.

I also feel that there are a lot of potential big-league ballplayers in the inner city, but I think there are too many big-league scouts who are afraid to go into those areas. I was talking to one of our scouts with the Cubs—Gary Hughes—about that topic and I told him that is what is happening.

There are places on the South Side of Chicago, such as Jackson Park, where kids are playing a good brand of baseball. But nobody from the major leagues watches them play unless they eventually get to play on a college campus.

The late Kirby Puckett, a Hall of Famer, and Curtis Granderson, an outstanding young ballplayer with the Detroit Tigers, were discovered after they were playing college ball. But they were outstanding young high school players in Chicago before that and nobody really noticed them.

So many of these young African American athletes need someone to talk to them the way Buck O'Neil talked to me when I got discouraged about playing baseball at the age of 18 or 19. Somebody has to tell them to be patient and believe in themselves, because great things could be there on the horizon if they hang in there.

This game of professional baseball is such a great life and these young players need to know that. We have one of the best pensions in all of professional sports. If you sign a contract and work hard and make it to the big leagues there are a lot of benefits you will receive. The rewards are greater than basketball and greater than football after you play in the big leagues for a certain amount of time.

Baseball is a game of failure. If you don't get a hit two out of three times, you are hitting .300 and doing a great job. You are not talking about getting a hit every time you come to bat. If you are hitting 2 out of 5 you are hitting .400 and you are a great player.

It's up to the young players to work hard. You know, Willie Mays worked hard, Hank Aaron worked hard...all of us had to work hard to get to the major leagues, even though we were to become Hall of Fame players.

CHAPTER 8

A Spoonful of Wheat Germ and Honey

Serving as the hitting coach for the Cubs from 1992–2001, I was afforded the unique opportunity to work with Sammy Sosa, the franchise's all-time leading home-run hitter and the only player in Major League Baseball history to have three seasons of at least 60 home runs.

The Cubs acquired Sosa in a trade with the Chicago White Sox in 1992. The Cubs sent George Bell to the Sox in exchange for him and pitcher Ken Patterson. I remember Sosa as a skinny kid with tremendous potential as a hitter, fielder, and base runner. He had a very strong arm in right field.

As a hitter, Sosa initially sprayed the ball well to all fields, but he did not display the raw power we all saw in the late 1990s and beyond. He eclipsed the 600-home-run mark in 2007 as a designated hitter with the Texas Rangers.

When he reported to the Cubs' spring training camp in Mesa in 1998, Sosa had bulked up to about 220 pounds and proudly showed off his well-chiseled biceps. He had hit 36 homers in 1997 and 40 in 1996. But in 1998, Sosa was off the chart with his power numbers. He drove in 158 runs, hit 66 homers, and had a slugging percentage of .647. Incredible numbers.

Ernie Banks's best season was in 1959 when he led the National League in RBIs with 143 and belted 43 home runs. Banks batted .304 with a .596 slugging percentage and 97 runs scored that year. Banks's all-time Cubs career home-run record of 512 was broken by Sosa in May of 2004.

Well, I have heard all of the rumors and speculation about Sosa using steroids or other performance enhancers. But nothing has been proven to this point, even though his change in appearance was rather sudden and conspicuous. When you look around the league these days, you see a lot of players whose appearances have changed dramatically.

When you look around the league these days, you see a lot of players whose appearances have changed dramatically.

A couple of years ago, Sosa told the *Chicago Tribune*, "I am clean and I have always been clean. There has been a lot of speculation, but they don't have evidence. So you take it from there. They haven't been writing a book about me doing this or doing that."

Word surfaced in 2006 that admitted steroid abuser Jason Grimsley implicated Roger Clemens, Andy Pettitte, and Miguel Tejada in a federal agent's affidavit.

In June of 2006, federal agents searched Grimsley's home in Arizona after the pitcher admitted using human growth hormone, steroids, and amphetamines. Grimsley later was released by the Arizona Diamondbacks and suspended for 50 games by Major League Baseball.

In a 20-page search warrant affidavit signed by IRS Special Agent Jeff Novitzky, Grimsley identified other players who had used drugs, according to the *Los Angeles*

Times. Those names were blacked out when the document was released.

The *Times* said an anonymous source with access to the document—minus the cross-outs—let the newspaper see it. The *Times* also said that a second source, who had identified the other players, provided additional details about the document. According to the affidavit, Grimsley told investigators Clemens and Pettitte "used athletic performance-enhancing drugs."

The affidavit also alleged Grimsley told federal agents that Brian Roberts, Jay Gibbons, and Tejada "took anabolic steroids."

Sosa, who played for the Orioles in 2005 with Grimsley, Tejada, Gibbons, and Roberts as teammates, was not implicated.

During my era, I struggled to maintain my weight at 173 pounds. For the life of me, I couldn't get up to 175.

I never talked to Sammy about his change in appearance. I just figured he had lifted weights and worked out extensively to achieve such heftiness. But I must admit that the change was rather dramatic.

The one other thing I noticed about Sammy was that along with his increase in upper body strength and home-run power came a decrease in his flexibility as a fielder and base runner. That seemed to be the tradeoff.

Sammy stole 22 bases in 1997 and 18 in 1998. He has not reached double figures in stolen bases since then. As a young player with the Cubs in 1993, he stole 36 bases. In 1995, he swiped 34.

Baseball commissioner Bud Selig summoned former senator George Mitchell to head up a committee to investigate steroid abuse in the league. If George Mitchell were to question me about Sosa, I would just say that I was naïve about steroid use. I just knew that the ball was really going out of the ballpark more and that players were getting bigger and stronger. I know that players today lift weights and do all kinds of things that we didn't when we played.

During my era, I struggled to maintain my weight at 173 pounds. For the life of me, I couldn't get up to 175. Now, if I had shown up at spring training weighing 215 or 220 pounds, people would have wondered what happened to my body and how I got there. If I had weighed 215 pounds, I don't think I would have been able to play in 1,117 straight games, either. I would have been carrying too much weight around.

I was able to hit 426 home runs during my career. And Banks cranked out 512 as a 175-pound string bean during a good part of his career. We both relied on quick wrists and great bat speed to generate home-run power.

It might sound strange, but the one thing that seemed to help me throughout my career was taking a spoonful of wheat germ and a spoonful of honey. I would take that day and night. And I think that helped me get through playing all of those day games. That is an old Southern remedy to keep folks from tiring. It worked for me. I guess you could call that my steroid alternative.

The heaviest thing I picked up during the off-season during my playing days was a bowling ball. We didn't have the time nor the facilities to train the way the players today can. A lot of the players today have gyms right in their own homes. When I was playing ball in the 1960s, we had to work another job during the off-season to support our families. We weren't making that much money as players.

While Sosa has remained unscathed thus far with regard to the steroid controversy, others such as Jason Giambi and Rafael Palmeiro have been proven guilty. Barry Bonds told a grand jury that he inadvertently used a cream and clear substance that was a steroid. He was facing a possible perjury charge.

I don't know that much about steroids, but I do know that steroids will not help you make contact with the baseball. I think the steroids must keep you at the top of your strength so that you can perform at your best level.

People have talked about Jose Canseco when he was with Oakland and then Texas. And we saw how Palmeiro told Congress that he had never used steroids before tests proved he had some in his system. I think that when you look at a player who is weighing about 175 or 180 pounds, then all of a sudden he comes into the next spring training at 220, it throws up a red flag.

There is no question that baseball fans love home runs. As the saying goes, "Chicks love the long ball." Turn on ESPN or any other sports network and highlights of the longest home runs are shown. In a lot of ways it seems as if Major League Baseball wants it both ways. They want to crack down on the use of performance enhancers, yet they promote the Home Run Derby competition during the All-Star break. The distance of the home runs is measured and reported to the fans and then celebrated.

At Miller Park in Milwaukee in 2002, Sosa blasted seven home runs that went 500 feet or more, nine that went 490 or more, and 10 that went at least 480 feet.

And Sosa didn't even win that Home Run Derby competition! The winner was Giambi, a few years before he admitted to using steroids.

People love to see the ball go out of the ballpark. I think that helps Major League Baseball and their advertisements. Folks want to see how far a baseball can be hit, and I think that emphasis can be misleading to a young kid. Because there are other ways to win a baseball game other than hitting the ball over the fence.

I hope baseball will get away from that overemphasis.

It might sound strange, but the one thing that seemed to help me throughout my career was taking a spoonful of wheat germ and a spoonful of honey.

Sosa was signed originally by the Texas Rangers before being traded to the White Sox in 1989. Charlie Lau had been his hitting coach for three years with the White Sox. Lau preached to all of his hitters to have a short, compact swing with an exaggerated follow-through. He wanted all of his hitters to use the same technique. He wanted to clone a lot of hitters, in my opinion. One of the standouts that Lau once worked with was the Kansas City Royals' George Brett, who was an American League batting champion. He was a great hitter and a Hall of Famer. But I believe that no two hitters are the same.

When Sosa came over to our club—the first day he joined the team in Arizona—I noticed that he swung at a pitch and missed it, then looked over at me in the dugout to check out my reaction. I looked out at him and pointed to the pitcher on the mound. I told Sammy to pay attention to what the pitcher is throwing, not what my reaction is to his swing. That was a habit he must have picked up with the White Sox and I had to straighten that out with him. I told him to finish his at-bat, then come over to me on the bench and we would talk about it.

Sammy was some kind of hitter and he had raw talent. He was quick, he was strong, and he feared nothing at the plate. He hit the ball hard to the opposite field in the gaps and he hit home runs to the opposite field. When he was swinging the bat well, he was keeping his head down and on the ball. I often reminded him of that because he was a low-ball hitter.

Sammy always wanted to go to the batting cage early, before batting practice would start officially. He was one of the guys who wanted special attention. That would be a time when Sammy and I would be down there near the cage alone and we would talk about different things. And our conversations weren't always about baseball. We would talk about different things in life. He comes from a tough area—San Pedro de Macoris, Dominican Republic. All of the people are very poor in that little town, and Sammy was a shoeshine boy trying to make a buck to help his family early in his life before he was discovered.

I got to know him more as a person than I did as a hitter during those early morning conversations. Sammy said his grandmother was the first person who really believed in him. His grandmother often told him that good things happen to good people. We would often talk about that down in the batting cage. I am also a believer in things happening for a reason and that good things happen to those who wait.

The ball started jumping off his bat because he was strong, quick, and had no fear. There were times, early in his stint with the Cubs, when Sammy would crowd the plate too much and pitchers could get him out by jamming him with a tailing fastball from a right-hander. So we had to correct that so he could extend his arms to drive through the baseball.

Sammy was always receptive to my advice as a hitting coach. I guess when you have credentials as a hitter like I do, players are more likely to listen. I served three stints as a coach with the Cubs: 1980–82, 1986–87, and 1992–2001. When I was a player, I respected the advice of a guy like Ted Williams, known as "The Splendid Splinter" and perhaps the greatest hitter of all time.

> The heaviest thing I picked up during the off-season during my playing days was a bowling ball.

One time when I was in Arizona during spring training as a player, I met Ted Williams on a golf driving range. We talked for a long time. You respect guys like that who have performed on the big-league level and done well. He was the last player to hit over .400 for an entire season.

Sosa had the great ability to hit, and I just critiqued it. Once he learned how to concentrate on all of the details of hitting, he really took off. He grasped how to hit. Sammy was a big fan of Roberto Clemente, the Hall of Fame right fielder with the Pittsburgh Pirates who was killed in a plane crash while trying to deliver supplies to earthquake disaster victims. Whenever we played the Pirates in Pittsburgh, I would try to gather up any pictures or other memorabilia related to Clemente and give them to Sammy because I knew that he idolized him.

While so much attention remained focused on Sosa throughout the 1998 season, I had to remind myself that I was the hitting coach for the entire Chicago Cubs team. You always have to incorporate the other players because you have got 25 guys. But when you have someone hitting more than 60 home runs a season, well...I like to hear that manager who says he treats all of his ballplayers the same way, because he is a liar. Everybody is not the same and, of course, you are going to do different things for that individual who carries the big workload. But I tried to work with everybody in the batting cage and talk to everybody and give them undivided attention. But there was a little extra for Sammy because he was having such great years for the Cubs. Some guys need that attention, some don't. Some guys need pats on the back and some need to be critiqued a little bit more.

Of the left-handed hitters that I worked with on the Cubs over the years, Mark Grace had the most natural and productive swing. He could put the ball in play and use the whole field. He was just a good hitter. He hit about .340, I believe, in the minors and I asked one of the other coaches if he could pull the ball. He learned how to pull the ball a little when he had to in the big leagues.

When Don Zimmer took over as the Cubs manager, he tried to get Grace to pull the ball more for power. Grace's batting average suffered a little bit. So he went back to being a contact hitter for higher average.

Grace's 16 seasons in the major leagues ended with an impressive .303 career batting average. Grace collected more hits (1,754) in the 1990s than any other player in the National League. He had a lifetime .329 batting average in the playoffs. A four-time Gold Glove fielder and three-time NL All-Star, the only aspect of Grace's game that likely will keep him out of the Hall of Fame is the fact he lacked great power for a first baseman, a traditional home-run-hitting position. Grace hit 511 doubles during his career, compared to 173 home runs.

When I was in the minors at Class AA San Antonio, my batting coach was Rogers Hornsby. When I first joined the Cubs we didn't have a hitting coach. We had Lew Fonseca, who came along to help us in about 1965 as a batting coach.

I told Sammy to pay attention to what the pitcher is throwing, not what my reaction is to his swing.

Hornsby would always talk about waiting for a good ball to hit. He would say, "The plate is 17 inches wide from your armpit to your knees." I would always keep that in my mind as a hitter. Wait for one good ball to hit and don't miss it.

A lot of us players watched each other as hitters and helped each other out in the early 1960s. Beckert, Santo, Ernie...we all knew to watch and help each other. We also used to watch film of us hitting for 15 or 20 minutes in the morning together.

The 1998 season was something to behold as Sosa and Mark McGwire of the St. Louis Cardinals waged an amazing assault on Roger Maris's 37-year-old home-run record of 61. As it turned out, they both eclipsed 61; McGwire wound up with 70 and Sosa had 66. Barry Bonds would then hit 73 homers in 2001 to establish the current one-season mark.

McGwire hit his 62nd home run off Steve Trachsel of the Cubs in 1998. The atmosphere in and around Busch Stadium in St. Louis was similar to a postseason game. There were so many writers and other media people down on the field before the game. It was a circus.

That particular year it was not at all uncommon for Sammy to hit two or three homers a game. Same thing for McGwire. The two of them really brought the interest of baseball back to the American public. It was so exciting.

A lot of media people were calling me day and night that year, asking me about Sammy, wanting to know what his secret was.

The scene in the Cubs locker room in 1998 always included a lot of friends and business associates of Sosa. The league had relaxed its rules on that sort of thing and many people who didn't really belong in the locker room had free access to it. Sammy's brother was a regular in the locker room and a lot of other people from the Dominican Republic were there a lot.

Major League Baseball subsequently decided to crack down on who had access to the locker room and that meant Sammy's entourage was excluded.

I can't recall any professional athlete in Chicago who had been more revered and praised than Sammy Sosa when he was hitting all of those home runs. In January of 1999 President Clinton invited Sosa to attend his State of the Union Address in Washington, D.C.

By the same token, I cannot recall any pro athlete who has since been as reviled by many sports fans and media in Chicago.

This was a guy who took the pressure off a lot of people in the Cubs organization because of the excitement he brought to the ballpark. Even when the Cubs were struggling to try to reach the .500 mark as a team, people filled the stands at Wrigley Field in hopes of seeing Sosa hit a home run. Some of his critics called Sosa a selfish player, yet he took the field every day unless he was seriously injured. He sprinted out to his position in right field and greeted the fans. He always had a smile on his face. He was just a likable guy.

There was a time in the mid-1990s when I was involved in a big meeting with the Cubs executives when they were contemplating trading Sosa. The team was not doing very well and Sammy was the team's most valuable commodity when it came to a trade.

I am also a believer in things happening for a reason and that good things happen to those who wait.

Everybody except former Cubs president Andy MacPhail wanted to get rid of Sosa. I stood up and said, "No, I see this kid playing for the Cubs and hitting a lot of home runs and doing all kinds of good things for us." This is what I could foresee from him. It was tough to see people turn on Sammy like that.

In the early '90s people came to the ballpark just to hear legendary Cubs broadcaster Harry Caray sing "Take Me Out to the Ball Game" and watch Sammy hit home runs. If Sammy had been taken out of the game before the seventh inning, fans would often leave the ballpark if we were already losing.

On the other hand, we could be losing by six or seven runs late in the game, but if they knew that Sammy was going to have another at-bat, the fans would stick around just to see that at-bat. They just wanted to see if he would hit another home run.

I don't know if people looked the other way when it came to steroids or not, but McGwire and Sosa certainly brought people into the ballpark.

The 1998 season was also exciting for Cubs fans because the team made the playoffs as a wild-card team, beating the San Francisco Giants in a one-game playoff at Wrigley Field.

That was an exciting time for the Cubs franchise. I remember that the day we won, our players were celebrating and shooting champagne on the fans at Wrigley Field. The late Rod Beck, who passed away in 2007, was so happy that night after doing the job in relief for us.

What a day and night that was for the Cubs and the Williams family. My daughter Julia had planned months before to have her wedding on that day. I remember leaving that wedding, dancing with my daughter at the reception, then going to the ballpark in my tuxedo.

Sosa followed up his 66-home-run season of 1998 with 63 homers in 1999 and 64 in 2001. He led the league in homers in 2000 with 50.

I was no longer the batting coach for the Cubs in 2003 when Sosa was caught using a corked bat.

Sosa's bat was shattered in the first inning of a game against Tampa Bay that year. He was ejected and subsequently suspended for eight games.

Sosa claimed he mistakenly picked up the corked bat he used to put on a show for fans during batting practice. He appealed and had the suspension reduced to seven games.

I was sitting at home watching the game that night with my grandson. It was the strangest thing. Sammy didn't need that corked bat because he was so strong that he could hit the ball far anyway. I don't know what made him do that.

My grandson, who had occasionally served as the Cubs' batboy, watched Tampa Bay catcher Toby Hall pick up the corked bat and hand it to the umpire. My grandson turned to me in our living room and said, "The catcher should have never picked up that bat. The Cubs' batboy should have gotten to it first."

But the point is: Sammy shouldn't have been using that corked bat. I said, "What the heck is going on?"

That incident sort of soured a lot of people on Sammy. That incident and the fact he left the ballpark early on the final day of the 2004 season.

Last year the *Chicago Tribune* reported that on the night Sosa's bat exploded with cork inside, officials from Major League Baseball notified the Cubs organization during the game that they had one hour to get rid of any other corked bats of Sosa's in the team's clubhouse before they came down to inspect his arsenal of bats. Supposedly, more than 70 marked corked bats then were extricated quickly by Cubs personnel from the clubhouse, about a third of them belonging to other players.

I was not personally made aware of that, but former Cubs player Tom Goodwin was quoted as saying that he had heard that story.

I do know that throughout the history of baseball, people have cheated. People have corked their bats to try to hit the ball farther than the next guy. Some players used to be able to have Super Balls inserted in their bats.

Sosa claimed he picked up the wrong bat that happened to be corked, but most hitters are very careful and particular about keeping up with their bats. I would have probably three bats in my locker when I was a player. I had one that was my game bat and the bat I would be using in batting practice...I would be getting that one ready for the game, just in case I broke the game bat. I would mark all of my bats to keep track of them. Sometimes I would take a can opener or something like that and groove the bat just a little bit.

Sosa said he used to use Rawlings, Louisville Slugger, and the X BAT when he was with the Cubs.

Sosa once told the *Chicago Tribune*, "I have three bats that I feel comfortable with that I keep in the dugout during the game. I have a game bat, and in case I break one of those, I replace it with another one. They feel about the same."

There were newspaper reports during the '90s that Grace and Sosa did not get along personally and that professional jealousy might have divided the Cubs locker room. Grace tried to quiet those rumors when the two were teammates. But after he joined the Diamondbacks Grace could not help but take a shot at Sosa when he was caught using a corked bat in 2003.

"Had I known when I played in Chicago there were corked bats in the bat rack, I probably would have hit 25 home runs," Grace was quoted as saying. "[Sosa] is going to have to answer a lot of questions. It's weird. Instead of hitting them 500 feet, he wants to hit them 550, I guess."

Nowadays even amphetamines, or "greenies" as we used to call them, are illegal in baseball. The league tests players for the presence of these chemicals in the players' bodies.

Amphetamines used to be present in every big-league locker room when I was playing ball. When I first came up to the big leagues, of course, they weren't illegal. They would give you extra strength. They would be sitting right there in a jar in the clubhouse for anybody to take. Over in Pittsburgh, the Pirates had a supplement that they called the "Red Juice" for players to take. And, later on, cocaine use was a widespread problem of members of their team and it became a big scandal.

Former Cardinals manager Whitey Herzog once said that about 30 percent of his players were using cocaine. Baseball is a game that has been around for a long time and a lot of elements come into it to try to destroy the game. Somehow, the game continues to survive.

I do know that throughout the history of base- ball, people have cheated. Steroid abuse today by some ballplayers makes it difficult for play- ers from my generation to assess what is going on in the current game. I know that Hank Aaron must feel con- flicted about having his all-time home-run record broken by Barry Bonds in 2007. I think all the players from the '50s and '60s realize that all of the records were made to be broken. But all of my contemporaries want to make sure that it was a legiti- mate breaking of the record. They want everything to be pure and on the up and up.

This is what the commissioner wants and this is what the people watching baseball want to see.

It is important that big-league ballplayers deliver the right message to young players just starting out in the game. I can imagine a young player starting out in Class A baseball seeing all of the home runs hit in the big leagues by players who have bulked up through illegal substances.

Those young guys might get the wrong impression and say, "I want to get stronger in a hurry so that I can hit more balls out of the ballpark and get all the publicity that they are getting."

A lot of the home runs that Ernie and I hit were line drives. They had to be because of the swirling wind at Wrigley Field, especially if you were a left-handed hitter like me. If you hit the ball on a line, then the wind didn't bother it too much. I broke Bill Nicholson's record for home runs as a left-handed Cubs hitter at Wrigley Field.

Bobby Murcer was acquired by the Cubs in 1977 when Bill Madlock was traded to the Giants. Murcer struggled to hit as many home runs as he thought he would in Wrigley Field. I have seen Murcer in recent years and he said to me, "I thought the wind blew out every day in Wrigley Field."

I jokingly said, "When Ernie and I left and retired, the wind started blowing in."

I realize that the shroud of steroid allegations surrounding sluggers such as Palmeiro, McGwire, Sosa, and Bonds makes it difficult for the sportswriters to decide when and if to vote them into the Hall of Fame.

There is certainly a question mark next to their names. Until this issue is cleared up, it will be difficult. If the writers vote them in right away, the voters will be criticized if the players did actually do something illegal. The other thing writers need to do, in my opinion, is determine exactly when the steroid use became illegal in baseball. They also need to examine what type of ballplayers these guys were before they allegedly began taking performance enhancers.

In other words, Barry Bonds was a terrific all-around ballplayer well before he allegedly began to take steroids. He was a base runner, a Gold Glove outfielder, and a great hitter. He has won seven Most Valuable Player awards in his career. I think you have to take that under consideration.

The irony is that all of these players accused of taking steroids already were very good ballplayers. I guess they wanted to be better than good. They wanted to be really outstanding.

The story circulating about Bonds is that he was jealous of the attention Sosa and McGwire were receiving in 1998 during their home-run record chase. I know that when Sosa played against the San Francisco Giants he had some of his best days because he knew Barry was on the field and he wanted to show off.

❧❧

In 1983, seven years after I had retired, the major league All-Star Game returned to Chicago. There was not the elaborate Home Run Derby competition, but they did have an old-timers' game. At the age of 45, I didn't consider myself an old-timer yet, but I was asked to play. I hit a pitch from the old Hall of Fame knuckleballer Hoyt Wilhelm and deposited it in the upper deck in right field. That homer got a lot of people buzzing. I knew I could still hit and hit for power.

The Cubs retired my No. 26 during a special ceremony on August 13, 1987. That was a beautiful day that I will never forget. That was the same year I was inducted into the National Baseball Hall of Fame, earning more than 85 percent of the sportswriters' votes.

Having my number retired and being inducted into the Hall the Fame really underscored to me how much my contributions to the game were appreciated—and helped me considerably in making the transition from player to observer and coach.

In looking back, I knew I wanted to play baseball and I wanted to be good. I think my life's plan worked out very well.

APPENDIX

Billy Williams Hall of Fame Induction Speech

Thank you. Thank you very much. Commissioner Ueberroth, my colleagues in the Hall of Fame, all those past and current players, guests, ladies and gentlemen, and baseball fans here, and across the world in other countries. Walking up here to receive this honor, and of course the recognition that goes on with it, reminds me of the first time that I came to the plate at the major league ball club. Then, as now, I may look fine on the outside but gee, my knees are weak. So you can just imagine how happy I was when, in 1960, I hit my first home run off the Los Angeles Dodgers, off of Stan Williams. Plus, the first home run was a game-winner and it all turned out real well, because after that first home run, 425 followed. That thrill, thank you, that thrill in 1960 was no match for the call I got on January the 14th. It started with a call from Jack Lang, who is the secretary-treasurer of the Baseball Writers' Association of America. And I think, "Through the past years, when Jack makes his call, he don't call up players and ask about the weather or health." And I think those words that Jack speaks for me in the six years of waiting, anxiety, and hope. I was really in the Hall of Fame and that's all that mattered to me at that time. As a 16-year member of the Chicago Cubs, I had become accustomed to waiting to hear that devisive phrase, "wait 'til next year." But at this time, I'm in the Hall of Fame and that's all that mattered to me. (applause) And I tell you when I got that call in January, it was beautiful because at that time I was able to share it with my wife Shirley—stand up, Shirley—(applause), my daughter Valarie (applause), my daughter Nina (applause), my daughter Julia (applause), my daughter Sandra (applause). As well as so many longtime fans who saw me perform in Chicago. (applause) Thank you. I was so excited that I had to call my father, Frank Susie Williams in Whistler, Alabama. And I can remember the time right after I got the call from Jack Lang, I immediately got on the phone and I said, "Dad, we made it. We're in the Hall of Fame." And it reminds me of a call I had to make 29 years earlier when I was called to the big leagues in Chicago. And I can remember doing the same thing, telling my father. I said, "Dad," after all the years, three and a half years I have played in the minor league, I think the ultimate goal is to play on a big league and I called and I said, "I'm here in Chicago. They gave me a Major League uniform and I'm here in the major leagues." (applause)

I can't overemphasize the gratitude I owe to my parents, who struggled in Whistler, Alabama. My dad unloaded banana boats to put food on the table and of course my mother did housework in the area to help ends meet. Together, they pointed me in the right direction and they showered my brothers and sisters with love, affection, guidance, and care. But at that time we didn't have very much money, but I think they could attest to most of the time we had other things. We were rich in spirit and we enjoyed each other. And we were proud. I wish my mother was here today to join in celebrating in this honor, but she's not, but I know she's here in spirit. Because she had such major roll especially in helping me develop my character so that I could deal with the ups and downs of life. But my brother Franklin—stand up Franklin—who played professional baseball with the Pittsburgh Pirates. (applause) Thank you. And my brother Adolph and Clyde who played semi-pro baseball. (applause) And my sister Vera, who is here. And they're all here to share this honor along with my Dad, who is watching now in Whistler, Alabama. Now here's the key, you Shirley, okay, are the unsung hero in my career. You've been a devoted friend and companion for more than 27 years. You were with me during my latter days in the minor leagues and of course throughout my professional career. Bringing comfort during troubled times and laughter during joyous moments. You enabled me to concentrate on baseball on those long road trips. You saw that the kids got their homework, got to school on time, clothed. You were there to counsel them with their problems and provided guidance when they needed it. Your assistance and cooperation was invaluable. I couldn't have made it without you. Okay. (applause)

And looking back over my baseball career, I can recall some great moments. Going high into the vines at Wrigley Field, catching a line drive off the bat of Henry Aaron to save a no-hitter for Kenny Holtzman. (applause) Coming in to make a shoestring catch to save another no-hitter for Milt Pappas. (applause) Hitting a home run, 1964 All-Star game, playing in 1,117 ball games. And earning me the nickname, "Iron Man." (applause) Receiving the batting title in 1972 and getting the joy of playing in six All-Star Games. (applause)

All of these milestones saw that I got help from a lot of great pitchers and it all began in 1956 with Ivy Griffin signing me to my first professional contract. And of course there was Buck O'Neil, when I was making my transition from the minor league to the Major League, who counseled and guided me through those adjustment periods. And there were the teammates I had in the '60s and in the '70s, who were some of the greatest. Especially the '69 ballclub. (applause) We batted as individuals and we played as a team. These and many people have made a great impact on my life. And in growing up, you always remember that one lady that when you was in grade school and her name was Lilly A. Dixon. I can remember from time to time Ms. Dixon would come in the classroom year after year and the words she repeats, "Good, better, best, never let it rest until the good is better and better is best." (applause) I knew the words meant nothing as a youngster, but year after year, they would surface, and become more and more pronounced as my career unfolds. By working hard, I wanted to be the best ballplayer in the big league. I put these words into action and worked hard and hard each year. These few words were the driving force behind my desire to succeed. And baseball, the measurement and pinnacle will and always be election to the Baseball Hall of Fame. And now that I'm here in the Hall of Fame I think I can say I'm one of the best. (applause) Along with 198 others who have been enshrined in this Hall since 1939, my election this year is of special importance to me. If it weren't for the courage of three great men, 40 years ago, I might not have the opportunity to have played 18 years in the big leagues and stand before you today. What occurred at that time took a deal of courage and a belief and ability of one man and of the righteousness and decision of the two others. In January 1947, the owners voted 15 to 1 to keep blacks from the Major Leagues. That vote led Branch Rickey, who was the president and owner of the Brooklyn Dodgers, to call Happy Chandler. Shortly after that phone call, history was made in a place called "The Cabin" in Versailles, Kentucky. During that meeting, they decided to bring Jackie Robinson into the major leagues, paving the way from the minority participation in America's greatest pastime. And it had nothing to do with the color of Jackie's skin, but all to do with his ability to play the game. (applause) All of this, of course, was proven in succeeding years by Jackie Robinson's outstanding performance on and off the field, and induction into baseball's Hall of Fame in 1962. This followed by the induction of Branch Rickey in 1967 and of Happy Chandler in 1982. All of these great men deserve thanks and gratitude for taking that courageous step. (applause) Two of them are no longer with us today, but I personally would like to thank you, Happy Chandler, (applause) for your outgoing and steadfast support in the game of baseball. Not only as Commissioner, but from year to year coming up here and getting involved in these annual ceremonies. Thank you, Sir. (applause)

The past 40 years have been difficult. But, it was laid, the ground was laid by such stars as Jackie Robinson, Larry Doby, Monte Irvin, who is with us, Satchel Paige, and others. As late as 1959, I could recall in Corpus Christi, Texas, when I couldn't eat at a lunch counter with the team. The owner told me to go around to the back if you want to eat in this restaurant and you eat in the kitchen by the stove. I was furious, but hungry. As we traveled up and down the highway on the road, I had to be taken to a private home. I couldn't stay at the hotel with the rest of the team. I think that most of you will agree, at this time, that wasn't right. (applause) Thank you.

These injustices wasn't fixed by Major League Baseball, they had to be fixed for all minorities years later by the government. This ceremony today is a reason to celebrate, but is also a time for reflection. A time to examine the game's strength and weakness, by improving what is good and correcting what is bad. (applause) Yes, the road is rocky and long, but the time to pave the way for true equality is now. The next courageous step rests with the owners of 26 Major League ballclubs. They can make the difference by not looking at the color of a man's skin, but by examining his ability, talent, knowledge, and leadership. (applause) If this is the land of opportunity, then let it be true to become the land of opportunity for all. Questions have been raised in recent months by the media about the participation of blacks and other minorities in decision-making positions in baseball. The issue wouldn't have come up if every job in baseball was open to every league, creed, race, and nationality. But this is not the case. We minorities, for the past four decades, have demonstrated our talents as players. And now we deserve the chance and consideration to demonstrate similar talents as third-base coaches, as managers, as general managers, as executives in the front office, and yes, owners of major league ballclubs themselves. (applause) Baseball has become considered America's favorite pastime. Now let's make this sport that reflects the true spirit of our great country and nation that more than 200 years ago was dedicated to the proposition that all men, all men are created equal. (applause)

Yes, plans and words can be transformed into actions and deeds. We ask for nothing less but we seek what is just. (applause) I know the experience I've had over the past years as a coach have helped me to prepare myself for the days when I'd be considered for a managerial or executive position with a major league ballclub.

I always set high goals for achievement and look forward to and welcome the challenge and opportunity. As I reflect on my life, I often think back to my mother's favorite hymn and it was "How Great Thou Art," which also has become a great hymn of mine. The words reflect the beauty of life and the appreciation each of us should have for this special blessing that is ours. And I've hummed them often because I thank the Almighty God for giving me the ability to play major league baseball and for protecting me over my 2,488 games. The opportunity to have made so many friends in this game of baseball. I know God is watching over us and contributing to this joyous occasion by granting us such a wonderful day. Thank you for joining me at this most precious time of my life. Thank you and thank you very much. (applause)